RENEW your MIND
with the POWER of THOUGHTS

Stephanie Jefferson

Renew Your Mind with the Power of Thoughts

First Print Edition
ISBN 13: 978-0692717004
Copyright © 2016 Stephanie Jefferson

This book is also available as an Ebook.

Stephanie Jefferson Ministries
www.StephanieJeffersonMin.org

www.RenewYourMindBook.com
feedback@RenewYourMindBook.com

CONTENTS

Acknowledgements

I would like to thank…

Darryl Jefferson, my husband and greatest supporter, who has changed my life in many wonderful ways. Thank you for encouraging me, believing in me, and for the countless sacrifices that you have made throughout my book-writing journey.

My mother, Mary L. Dobbs, my first teacher, who has always believed in me and encouraged me throughout my life.

My children, Alonzo, Alondria and Aliyah Baker, the source of my inspiration. Thank you all for supporting and encouraging me along the way.

My pastor, Dr. Bill Winston. Thank you for teaching and guiding me towards spiritual growth.

To all of my family members, friends, and colleagues who continue to support me and offer kind words of encouragement. Thank you all for the love and respect. May God continue to bless and enlarge you all. What God starts, he will finish. Nothing can stop the plan and power of God!

Dedication

I would like to dedicate this book to the loving memory of my father, Mr. Robert Dobbs Sr., who has been my world and to the body of Christ that your mind might be renewed and restored.

Introduction

The Lord placed a scripture in my heart that ignited a ministry on warfare, strongholds and deliverance.

> **"For though we walk in the flesh, we do not war after the flesh: for the weapons of our warfare are not carnal, but mighty through God to the pulling down of strongholds;) casting down imaginations, and every high thing that exalteth itself against the knowledge of God, and bringing into captivity every thought to the obedience of Christ"**

> **- 2 Corinthians 10: 3-5**

This scripture is the launching pad that leads to a deeper understanding of spiritual warfare and evokes us to think about the source of our thoughts, and how our thoughts and beliefs influence our life and behavior. It was this scripture that the Holy Spirit repeatedly whispered to my spirit that eventually set a blaze of fire in my heart that led me to write this book. This scripture is the foundation of my ministry and unfold many critical topics that will catapult readers to transformation and spiritual victory. After much meditation and study, I realized that God had placed an urgent, powerful message in my heart about warfare in the mind. Although I do not claim to be a scientist or brain expert, my research has led me to some life-changing knowledge that I am thrilled to share with the body of Christ. Readers will gain wisdom about strongholds and how to break the power over their lives. Readers will also obtain insight on childhood programs, which include belief systems and behavior patterns that are affecting their lives today, how to re-write negative programs and how to increase their faith to manifest the promises of God in their lives.

This book is written for those who want to learn how to recognize and pull down faulty thinking patterns, identify strongholds, and train the subconscious mind God's way.

If you want practical, knowledge for how to change your beliefs, here they are in this Holy Spirit inspired, easy read, easy to understand writing for everyone on recognizing the signs of strongholds, reprogramming and renewing your mind. This book covers the necessary components that you need to break through to the next level of making the promises of God a reality in your life. Read with an expectation and confidence that every stronghold in your mind will be broken, demolished and shattered to pieces as you experience the power of renewing and rewriting beliefs in your mind with the power of your thoughts.

Chapter One

STRONGHOLDS

The Greek word for stronghold is *ochyroma*. The word stronghold means fortress. Some translate strongholds as prisons. Strongholds can be physical, emotional, or psychological. A stronghold is an influence by Satan over a certain area of a person's life. A stronghold is a place in a person's mind where negative thoughts, negative attitudes, and sinful habits are protected by Satan, the strongman, and his demons. These strongholds include lies and beliefs that come against the true understanding and knowledge of God.

Strongholds hold us strong and rob us of the abundant life that God had originally planned for our lives. Strongholds, once they are built in a person's life, are supported by excuses and reasons that one makes to justify his behavior and beliefs about life. Strongholds are behavior patterns and faulty thinking patterns that most people deny they have a problem with, which prevents them from receiving the truth and freedom that comes from the word of God. The lies that one believe, wrong behavior patterns, and sinful habits are like strong, fortified walls that act as a barrier, which blocks God's love and truth from penetrating and entering into a person's heart and transforming their lives. Many of us have seen this when we are trying to encourage someone to do the right thing or convince someone that a behavior is not right. When we are not able to convince someone about his or her behavior or choices in life, some of us say, "I feel like I was talking to a brick wall." A stronghold is like that. You cannot get through to a person's mind to bring the truth of God's word in because there is a stronghold, a strong wall that will not allow God's truth to come in.

"The thief cometh not, but for to steal, and to kill, and to destroy..." (John 10:10). Strongholds are strategically designed to limit, defeat, restrict, hinder, destroy, steal your inheritance, ruin your health, draw you away from God's truth, keep you lost, steal your dream and future, keep you in bondage, and prevent you from moving forward and advancing in life.

"When a strongman armed keepeth his palace, his good are in peace" (Luke 11:21). The strongman is the devil. He

2

is armed with all sorts of devious schemes such as temptations, deception, and accusations that lead to strongholds and bondage. His palace (home) is inside of the hearts of unsaved, un-renewed minds of men. The strongman's goods are all of the good things in life that God freely gives to us, which includes good health, wealth, marriage, children, family, sound mind, peace, joy, your life, and anything that is of value to you. The strongman's good are the things that Satan has stolen from someone. Once the strongman steals your things, Satan and his demons guard and protect them with great care. Their job is to deceive you and keep you blind as they continue to rob, steal and destroy your life.

The goods, that they have stolen are in peace, unmoved and unclaimed, because Satan has blinded the minds of unbelievers, and many do not even know that their possessions have even been stolen. Satan's palace, his home, is inside of the unbeliever's heart. Sadly and in many cases, unbelievers are unaware that they have been robbed, in bondage and living in darkness until it is too late. How can you recognize a stronghold if you don't know what a stronghold is? In order to recognize a stronghold, you must first understand what a stronghold is and how Satan's use of deception keeps you blind and lost. 2 Corinthians 4:3-4 tells us why a person's mind may not be renewed.

"But if our gospel be hid, it is hid to them that are lost: In whom the god of this world hath blinded the minds of them that believe not…"

What stronghold is Satan and his demons using to drag you down? What is weighing you down and holding you back? What has the strongman stolen from you?

It is not very difficult to recognize and name a stronghold. Recognizing a stronghold is as simple as calling it by what it is. What area(s) in your life are you having trouble in? What is holding you strong? Calling it by its name is how you can immediately recognize and detect a stronghold or the Strongman that has a grip on you: addiction, sexual immorality, anger, jealousy, unforgiveness, depression, sickness, poverty, etc.…

Satan is the God of this world. He influences the world and controls it by putting negative images on television, social media, and inside of books to control, manipulate, and distort the mind, thoughts and behavior of those who do not obey and believe the word of God. 1 John 2:15 tells us,

"Love not the world, neither the things that are in the world. If any man loves the world, the love of the Father is not in him. For all that is in the word, the lust of the flesh, and the lust of the eyes, and the pride of life, is not of the Father, but is of the world."

Once you open the door of sin to Satan and his demons, you give them legal authority to come in. Once they get in, they will be able to do whatever they want, which is to ultimately destroy your life.

Strongholds are demonic, evil spirits that control the lives of those who fall into captivity by opening doors to various, insidious, spirits. Consider them as evil quests- visitors who come in and make their home inside of your body. A strongman is a head, high-ranking ruler spirit that sits on thrones in the spirit realm and rules over all other evil spirits that operate in the earth realm. These evil spirits are powerful forces that hinder our prayers and deliverance. To get rid of evil spirits, you must first deal with the strongman.

The Bible speaks of 16 demonic strongman sprits. These sprits includes the Spirit of Divination, Familiar Sprit, Spirit of Jealousy, Lying Spirit, Perverse Spirit, Spirit of Haughtiness, Spirit of Heaviness, Spirit of Whoredom, Spirit of Infirmity, Deaf and Dumb Spirit, Spirit of Bondage, Spirit of Fear, Seducing Spirits, Spirit of the Anti-Christ, Spirit of Error, and Sprit of Death. In order to be free from these strongmen, deliverance must take place. It is written that when a strongman is fully armed and guards his palace, his possessions are safe until someone else who is stronger over takes him. Jesus is undeniably stronger than the strongman, and He is ready to deliver you!

We know that these strongholds did not come from God, **"For God hath not given us the spirit of fear; but of power, and of love, and of a sound mind"** (2 Timothy 1:7). We must be on guard and learn how to recognize strongholds and tear them down with the power of God before they can be built, fortified, embedded in our minds and accepted as a way of life.

It is time to bind up the strongman and stop allowing him to defeat you. God gave you power and authority. There is power in the name of Jesus. There is power in the blood of Jesus. There is power in the word of God. You have been given authority to use the name of Jesus, His blood, and God's word against all the power of darkness.

> **"Behold, I give unto you power to tread on serpents and scorpions, and over all the power of the enemy: and nothing shall by any means hurt you"** (Luke 10:19)

God's word is powerful. His word is the seed that brings life, healing, health, and destruction to strongholds. Plant His word in your heart, renew your mind daily and as you confess and believe, your faith will cause God's word to grow and manifest in your life. In Psalms 107:20, we are told, **"He sent his word, healed them, and delivered them from their destructions."** Every time we speak, confess, and believe God's word in faith, the power of healing and deliverance are available to us. God gave us the keys to receive his power and to regain access to take back everything that the strongman, the devil, has stolen from us.

"And I will give unto thee the keys of the Kingdom of heaven: and whatsoever thou shalt bind on earth shall be bound in heaven: and whatsoever thou shalt loose on earth shall be loosed in heaven" (Matthew 18:18)

Jesus has given us power and authority over the strongman and his demons to stop them from operating while we pray for the Holy Spirit to bring us life, remove the chains and set us free. To bind is to forbid, pronouncing something as unlawful. You have been given power and authority to stop Satan in his tracks. Because God gave us keys, we have legal rights to stop the strongman. Binding the enemy stops, paralyzes, and temporarily arrests Satan and his demons, which stops them from further operating in our lives. Loosening gives us power to release the power of God's word on earth to receive the help that we need. Yes, when God gave us the keys to the kingdom, he gave us authority to open doors of faith, healing and deliverance and to close doors to Satan and his demons. Use your keys (name of Jesus, blood of Jesus, Word of God, and the power of your faith) to manifest the miraculous power of God!

"Let us search and try our ways, and turn again to the Lord" (Lamentation 3:40). God wants to transform us. Attending church service week after week, month after month, and year after year without being transformed is as absurd as going to a gym week after week, month after month and year after year without your body being transformed. We are no threat to Satan and his kingdom as long as we attend church without searching our hearts, not being delivered from strongholds and being transformed. We must continually examine our lifestyles, hearts, attitudes, thoughts, and beliefs if we are going to have spiritual victory and success as God intends for us to have. No longer should we be content with going to church services without expecting healing and deliverance from strongholds.

Unfortunately, so many believers attend church but their lives, attitudes, behavior, and beliefs never change. Recognizing the signs of strongholds and being honest with yourself are a necessary and critical steps toward obtaining true freedom and deliverance. Renewing the mind will bring change. Renewing your mind is not something you do once a week or whenever you feel like it. Renewing your mind is a lifelong, daily process, and should be done daily to keep your mind and thoughts in harmony with the promises and thoughts of God.

Just like our cell phones and electronic gadgets need to be charged daily, so does our mind. We need to stay connected and plugged into the word of God. **"…it is written, Man shall not live by bread alone, but by every word that proceeded out of the mouth of God"** (Matthew 4:4). Galatians 5:19-21 is a great place to start this search within our hearts and minds. When we operate from our flesh, strongholds are built. The longer we practice the works of the flesh, the stronger the stronghold gets.

What is holding you? Who or what is stopping you? It is time to break free from the strongman and take back your belongings! Stand up today and fight for what belongs to you. Take back everything that has been taken from you by faith and reclaim the victorious life and original plan of God for your life!

God is a restorer!

> **"And I will restore to you the years that the locust hath eaten, the cankerworm, and caterpillar, and the palmerworm, my great army which I sent among you"** (Joel 2:25)

The Hebrew origin of these four insects represent a type of locust at a different stage of development: larvae, young locust, non-winged, and winged represent the progression of sin and how not addressing it causes it to spiral out of control, devour and destroy our lives. God is able to restore everything that the devil has stolen from you, but restoration begins when repentance takes place and strongholds are destroyed. Let the power of God destroy your stronghold.

The power of God is stronger than any strongman, demon or stronghold. Although Strongholds are powerful, dangerous and destructive, we can rely on the unfailing, supernatural power of God to deliver us!

"But when a stronger than he shall come upon him, and overcome him, he taketh from him all his armor wherein he trusted, and divideth his spoils" (Luke 11:22)

On March 18, 2012, I experienced the miraculous, awesome divine hand and supernatural power of deliverance as I was instantly delivered from a 15-year stronghold of addiction to nicotine. A couple of weeks before my deliverance, I sat down and wrote out a goal, which expressed my desire and date that I wanted to commit to quit. Needless to say, but I have tried, on my own, and failed miserably several times as I wrestle with my stronghold of addiction. My hour of deliverance came during a regular but powerful Sunday morning service. My pastor, Dr. Bill Winston was teaching. He started to cry out for the congregation. When he said the following words, "You didn't know…" the power of God was demonstrated in my life, and the stronghold of addiction was instantly broken off me and destroyed! Immediately, I knew that I was free from a stronghold that had plagued and held me captive for many, many hopeless years. If I had to describe the feeling I had during my hour of deliverance, I would say that in a moment it felt like a door was unlocked, opened, chains fell off, and I was able to walk away freely without any questions. **"Now unto him that is able to do exceeding abundantly above all that we ask or think, according to the power that worketh in us"** (Ephesians 3:20). Your hopeless situation is no match for God.

"Who hath delivered us from the power of darkness, and hath translated us into the kingdom of his dear son" (Colossians 1:13). Only God can deliver us from the powerful grip of darkness. If you do not allow or have the desire for God to destroy your stronghold, your stronghold will ultimately destroy you. Do you want to be delivered? Let God pull down your strongholds. In Galatians 5:19-21, as you identify and begin to discover strongholds in your life, repent to God, renounce your sins, resist the devil as you are set free, renew and reprogram your mind with the word of God.

Repent means to renounce sin. Webster's dictionary defines repent as: "to turn from sin, to feel regret, to change one's mind, and to feel sorrow for." The parable of the Prodigal son shows that when the son repented, he did not stay in the same environment with the pigs, but he got up and left. When we repent, there must be a turning away from something: negative thoughts, sinful habits, or negative beliefs and behaviors. Synonyms for repent include: apologize, be sorry, feel remorse, regret and sorrow.

Just "feeling" sorry for our sinful behavior is not enough. Sincere repentance leads to a change in our thoughts, beliefs and behavior. When repenting from our sin, strongholds such as poverty, drug addiction and sexual immorality, depression, divorce, alcoholism, infirmity, anger and perversion are usually past down within a family bloodline from generation to generation as a curse. Generational curses are curses

11

brought on by the sins of our forefathers and foremothers back to the 3rd, 4th, and even the 10th generation. All families have spiritual traits that are passed down through the family bloodline also known as familiar spirits. As you ask for forgiveness of your sin(s), renounce the sins of your fathers, forefathers, mothers and grandmothers' sin. Below includes a prayer of repentance:

Heavenly Father, I come to you in the name of Jesus to ask you to forgive me for *(Be specific in your request: sexual immorality, drinking, smoking, gossip, unforgiveness, etc...)* I repent and renounce *(sexual sins, pornography, drugs, alcohol, nicotine, jealousy, strife, anger, hatred, gossip, lying, murder, bitterness, mental illness, suicide, grief, and all other compulsive behaviors)* In the name of Jesus, I repent of my sins and the sins of my forefathers and foremothers back to the 3rd, 4th, and even the 10th generation. I renounce each of these sins and plead the blood of Jesus over myself and over my family bloodline all the way down the tenth generation. I decree and declare that I am blessed and not cursed because Christ has redeemed me from the curse of the law. Now unto God who is able to do exceeding, abundantly above all I could ask or think of concerning every area of my life. Thank you, Father for cleansing, healing and setting me free. I believe and receive my deliverance in the name of Jesus Christ. Amen.

"Resist the devil and he will flee from you. Draw nigh to God, and he will draw neigh to you" (James 4: 7-8). Draw near to God through renewing your mind, spending time in the word, and God will draw near to you. We can resist the devil by not allowing ourselves to yield to the fiery darts of negative thoughts that he constantly bombard our minds with. We can resist the devil as we choose not to tolerate the sins of our ancestors. We can resist the devil by staying in the word of God as we renew our minds daily. Your faith, prayer and the word of God are powerful weapons of resistance and should be used daily to resist temptation and deception from Satan.

"What? Know ye not that your body is the temple of the Holy Ghost which is in you, which ye have of God, and ye are not your own? For ye are bought with a price: therefore, glory God in your body, and in your spirit, which are God's" (1 Corinthians 6:19-20)

Once you renew your mind with the word of God, you will establish healthier programs that will empower you to live according to the original plan of God for your life. Instead of stronghold getting stronger, you can live a stronghold free life. Many people do not realize that although we gather to worship God in a church, we are the church! Our body is the temple of God. Let us honor God and live our lives in such a way that glorifies God in how we keep and present ourselves. **"I beseech you therefore, brethren, by the mercies of God, that ye present yourself a living sacrifice, holy, acceptable**

unto God, which is your reasonable service" (Romans 12:1). Present yourself! That sounds exactly like something that a loving father would say to his child.

The final step toward freedom in your deliverance includes being filled with the life changing power of the Holy Spirit. We are not, on our own, able to live and walk in the fullness of God without the presence and power of the Holy Spirit. If you have the desire to be a doer of God's word, you are going to need some help.

> **"Howbeit when he, the Spirit of truth is come, he will guide you into all truth: for he shall not speak of himself; but whatsoever he shall hear, that shall he speak: and he will shew you things to come"** (John 16:13)

The Holy Spirit is your invisible but present helper, teacher, comforter, and He will lead and guide you to all truth. The Holy Spirit has been my personal navigator in life and my personal, built-in, internal alarm system. Personally, I have had and continue to have many life-changing and powerful experiences with the Holy Spirit. God is so kind, gracious, merciful, and He sends his messages of hope, love and peace through the Holy Spirit. If you do not know, the Holy Spirit is not an It. He is a Divine Person. He is the third Person of the Trinity. There is one God represented in three persons: God the Father, God the Son and God the Holy Spirit. The Holy Spirit is your helper, teacher, and comforter. He will lead and guide you from day to day, if you allow him. He has done some incredible things in my life and continues to empower and lead me daily. The Holy Spirit has gently nudged my heart, alerted my spirit when my thoughts, beliefs or behavior were out of line with the word of God. The Holy Spirit checks my spirit and keeps me in line when my flesh rises and reminds me to walk in peace, forgiveness and in love. The Holy Spirit empowers me to operate in the fruit of the spirit: love, joy, peace, longsuffering, gentleness, goodness, faith, meekness and temperance. He leads me throughout my day as a navigator and tells me what to do, say, and where to go. On several occasions, the Holy Spirit has alerted me when I was not in good company; my spirit knows when I encounter evil spirits as well as good spirits. On other occasion, the Holy Spirit has prompted me to keep some conversations short and not reveal too much information to certain people concerning my life and future plans. He is my spiritual antenna and is always clearly tuned in to anything that is a threat to my wellbeing. Allow the Holy Spirit to lead, guide, protect and help you.

Another one of the Holy Spirit's jobs is to also remind you of God's word and to give you personal messages sent directly from God. I have had several encounters with the Holy Spirit, and I have received messages, in a time of need, directly from God, Himself! Like David, the Psalmist said, **"In my distress, I called upon the Lord: he heard my voice out of his temple, and my cry came before him, even into his** ears" (Psalms 18:6). During my personal time of distress, I, too, cried out to the Lord and asked him to help me. I was in a hopeless situation and felt as if my life was drowning in the Red Sea of hopelessness. As I cried out to God, I lifted up my hand as an act of my dependence in him to help me. Before I could take my hand down, I clearly heard a still, small voice whisper, "Jeremiah 29:11." Before this encounter, I had never read that scripture before. This was God's personal message to me:

> **"For I know that thoughts that I think toward you, said the Lord, thoughts of peace, and not of evil, to give you an expected end. Then shall ye call upon me, and ye shall go and pray unto me, and I will hearken unto you. And ye shall seek me, and find me, when ye search for me with all your heart. And I will be found of you, saith the Lord: and I will turn away your captivity, and I will gather you from all the nations, and from all the places whither I have driven you, said the Lord; and I will bring you again into the place whence I caused you to be carried away captive"** (Jeremiah 29:11-14).

What a timely and very comforting word to receive during a time of hopelessness in my life. Hallelujah! You can imagine how I must have felt to turn to this scripture and read those words of assurance, peace and comfort. As my pastor, Dr. Bill Winston says, "One word from God can change your whole life."

Another encounter I had with a direct word from God through the Holy Spirit was regarding paying my tithes. Although I am a faithful tither, on this particular occasion, I was reasoning with myself as I was debating delaying my tithe. During my personal debate, I heard this scripture playing repeatedly in my head, in the form of a song: *Will a man rob God? Will a man rob God? Will a man rob God?* (Malachi 3:8). This is a humorous example of how God speaks directly to us concerning matters that we may not want to hear about. Jesus said, **"But ye shall receive power, after that the Holy Ghost is come upon you…"** (Acts 1:8). If you have not already been filled with the Holy Spirit, ask God and by faith, just receive it.

"If you then, being evil, know how to give good gifts unto your children: how much more shall your heavenly father give the Holy Spirit to them that ask him?" (Luke 11:13)

God loves to give us good gifts just as much as we love to give our children good gifts. Ask the Lord to fill you with the Holy Spirit and you will soon discover that you have invisible help.

"Now unto him that is able to do exceeding abundantly above all that we ask or think, according to the power that worketh in us" (Ephesians 3:20). With the help from the Holy Spirit, the urge for nicotine no longer has dominion over me. I received the power I need to resist the urge to sin.

I am no longer a slave to nicotine. The stronghold of addiction is no longer my master **"Let not sin therefore reign in your mortal body, that ye should obey it in the lusts thereof"** (Romans 6:12). Only God can deliver you from the evil grip of strongholds and the power of the Holy Spirit is able to keep you from falling back into sin.

> **"There hath not temptation taken you but such as common to man: but God is faithful, who will not suffer you to be tempted above that ye are able; but with the temptation also make a way to escape, that ye may be able to bear it"** (1 Corinthians 10:13)

Get connected to the power of the Holy Spirit; your life will never be the same!

"Now unto him who is able to keep you from falling, and to present you faultless before the presence of his glory with exceeding joy" (Jude 24:25). It is my prayer that the Lord will answer by fire, pull down every demonic stronghold, and burn them to ashes with his awesome presence and all-consuming power. In the name of Jesus Christ, I break the power of darkness over your life, and I command every demonic chain of bondage related to the strongholds of addictions, wrong thoughts, and wrong attitudes to be broken by the power of God. Loose your hold and let go, now! In the name of Jesus Christ, I decree that you are delivered and free. Whom the Son sets free is free indeed. **"Stand fast therefore in the liberty wherewith**

Christ has made us free, and be not entangled again with the yolk of bondage" (Galatian 4: 10)

Chapter Two

BOOT CAMP
Preparing for the Battle

———•═══•———

Hut 2, 3, 4! Are you ready? The thief is coming without a doubt, and there is an invisible but real battle going on in the spirit for your soul. In 2 Corinthians 10:3, we are told that we are in a war, **"For though we walk in the flesh, we do not war after the flesh."** The war that we are in is not one that can be seen with the natural eye. We are fighting invisible, evil spirits from the kingdom of darkness who oppose the things of God. The place where the battle is taking place is inside of our mind and begins within our thoughts. You have heard statements like, "You have been programmed."

Understanding the origins and nature of programs are another important part that will prepare you for this battle, help you understand the nature of your thoughts, how they shape your belief systems, how your belief systems affect your behavior and how your thoughts continue to influence and control your life today.

What is a program, and how does one become programmed? A program or programs are genetically and environmentally coded instructions that you unconsciously learn, from conception up until about the age of seven, for how to respond to your environment and how to deal with various situations in life. You subconsciously inherited the beliefs that control and affect you. These programs tell you what to do or how to act or react during various situations in your life. As a result of programming, you can drive, communicate and take care of your daily needs. After the age of seven, although we continue to learn from those who we were around the most, we learn primarily through repetition and reinforcement. I will discuss more on this in later chapters.

When it comes to thoughts, most of our thoughts come directly from our spiritual enemy, and we struggle or battle with them constantly. Our enemy is Satan, the Strongman, and his demons. His objective is to do three things: kill, steal and destroy us. His goal is to accomplish this by sending temptation, deception and accusation our way. We can be tempted to accept and believe negative thoughts. Those negative thoughts are rooted in deception and lies that lead to attitudes that influence our behavior towards God or towards others in a negative way. Satan and his helpers are always lurking and seeking whom they can ensnare, hold captive, control, and devour.

Renewing your mind is a prerequisite as you prepare and enter into the battlefield of your mind. As we renew our minds, we find specific instructions on how to overcome every force of evil. God has equipped believers with his armor, his weapons, providing everything they need and therefore, as a believer, you have an advantage over our adversary.

"Lest Satan should get an advantage of us: for we are not ignorant of his devices" (2 Corinthians 2: 11). Webster's Dictionary defines device as such: Something that is done in order to achieve a particular effect. A plan, technique, a scheme to deceive: stratagem, trick. Our enemy is strategic and through his carefully devised temptation, deception and accusation, he operates with a clever and often dishonest plan to do or get something. Satan wants you to think or believe things that are not true, and that is why he starts war with us through the thoughts that he send into our mind. He wants to deceive you. His deception leads to sin and causes us to be trapped and controlled by him and his officer demons. When I first started smoking cigarettes, I never imagined that when "I" wanted to quit, I would not be able to. After opening up a door to Satan, I became his servant and prisoner. I became a slave to nicotine, and the nicotine had become my master. It was no longer I that was 'in control" of the nicotine, but the nicotine was in control over me, making me do something that I no longer wanted to do. I was smoking against MY will. Romans 6:16 tells us, **"Know ye not that to whom yield yourselves servants to obey, his servants ye are to whom ye obey…"** Satan is plotting on YOU. No two plans are the same. He plots on each of us and carefully create well thought out, custom made plans that are uniquely and specifically designed to trap every one of us. In Luke 4, 1-13, he plotted on Jesus and tried to tempt Him three times.

"And Jesus being full of the Holy Ghost returned from Jordan, and was led by the Spirit into the wilderness, Being forty days tempted of the devil. And in those days he did eat nothing: and when they were ended, he afterward hungered. And the devil said unto him, If thou be the Son of God, command this stone that it be made bread. And Jesus answered him, saying, It is written, That man shall not live by bread alone, but by every word of God. And the devil, taking him up into an high mountain, shewed unto him all the kingdoms of the world in a moment of time. And the devil said unto him, All this power will I give thee, and the glory of them: for that is delivered unto me; and to whomsoever I will I give it. If thou therefore wilt worship me, all shall be thine. And Jesus answered and said unto him, Get thee behind me, Satan: for it is written, Thou shalt worship the Lord

thy God, and him only shalt thou serve. And he brought him to Jerusalem, and set him on a pinnacle of the temple, and said unto him, If thou be the Son of God, cast thyself down from hence: For it is written, He shall give his angels charge over thee, to keep thee: And in their hands they shall bear thee up, lest at any time thou dash thy foot against a stone. And Jesus answering said unto him, It is said, Thou shalt not tempt the Lord thy God. And when the devil had ended all the temptation, he departed from him for a season."

In Genesis 3 1-6, Satan deceived Eve:

Now the serpent was more subtle than any beast of the field which the Lord God had made. And he said unto the woman, Yea, hath God said, Ye shall not eat of every tree of the garden? And the woman said unto the serpent, We may eat of the fruit of the trees of the garden: But of the fruit of the tree which is in the midst of the garden, God hath said, Ye shall not eat of it, neither shall ye touch it, lest ye die. And the serpent said unto the woman, Ye shall not surely die: For God doth know that in the day ye eat thereof, then your eyes shall be opened, and ye shall be as gods, knowing good and evil. And when the woman saw that the tree was good for food, and that it was pleasant to the eyes, and a tree to be desired to make one wise, she took of

the fruit thereof, and did eat, and gave also unto her husband with her; and he did eat.

Like Eve, so many people are deceived and believe Satan's lies, which lead many out of the will of God and into captivity. I have seen so many people, especially young people, suffer because they did not know that they were being spiritually violated and held against their will. Rebellion and disobedience keep us from God's truth and deliverance against the kingdom of darkness. Satan and his demons capitalize on the strong-willed, rebellious, disobedient nature of teens and young adults. Because most of them do not know what a stronghold is, they do not realize that they are being held captive. Throughout the Bible, there are several examples of people who chose to do things their way and how their rebellion and disobedience to God led to negative consequences:

- Adam and Eve were put out the Garden of Eve because they disobeyed God (Genesis 3).

- Moses was not able, as originally planned, to lead the Children of Israel to the Promise Land because he disobeyed God (Numbers 20).

- The Children of Israel wondered in the wilderness for 40 years until all the generation that had done evil in the sight of the Lord was dead because they were stubborn, disobedient, rebellious and unfaithful. (Exodus 3: 2-9) (Exodus 33:3) (Deuteronomy 9:7, 24, 27)

- King Saul was rejected by God and God choose another king because Saul disobeyed God (1Samuel 15:22).

- Jonah was swallowed up by a great fish for three days and three nights because he disobeyed God (Jonah 1:17).

Revelation 12:10 tells us, **"For the accuser of our brethren is cast down which accused them before our God day and night."** This is why character and integrity are critical in Christian living. Character is the combination of morals and beliefs that dictates our behavior, how we treat others, our environment and ourselves. Developing sound character and integrity are critical elements as we enter into battle. A life without integrity can hinder our faith and walk with God and allow the enemy to come in to defeat us. Webster Dictionary defines character as: *"the way someone thinks, feels, and behaves: someone's personality."* Integrity is defined as *"being honest and fair."* It is who we are when no one is watching. The book of Proverbs is a great place to renew your mind for areas of your life concerning character, personal conduct, sexual relations, revenge, wealth, childrearing, business, discipline, charity and alcohol, to name a few.

"That ye may be blameless and harmless, the sons of god, without rebuke, in the midst of a crooked and perverse nation, among whom ye shine as lights in the world" (Philippians 2:14)

Character is how people see you. Integrity is how you see yourself, the true you. The accuser of the brother is always trying to find fault with you, get others to find fault with you and to poison our relationships with one another. He is always looking for reasons to keep you from getting to your promise land. Let your light shine everywhere you go; do not get tired to doing good. **"And let us not be weary in well doing: for in due season we shall reap if we faint not"** (Galatians 6:9).

Finally, we are told how to dress for this battle and who we are battling with.

> **"Put on the whole armor of God that ye may be able to stand against the wiles of the devil. For we wrestle not against flesh and blood, but against principalities, against powers, against the rulers of darkness of this world against spiritual wickedness in high places"** (Ephesians 6:11-12)

Satan has an organized army. He is armed and dangerous, and you need to understand how he operates. Satan and his high-ranking demons are powerful, dangerous, and we should not minimize their power and influence in the earth. We wrestle with evil spirits inside of a human body who is influenced by Satan and his dark kingdom. Have you ever seen someone who is mean, rude, and impolite for no apparent reason? Have you ever wondered how one person can kill another? Have you ever experienced warfare, hostility and strife in your home, your workplace, grocery store, or in traffic? People who perpetuate evil acts towards others are being used by the devil and most people do not really know that they are being used. It is not the person that is evil, but the spirit that is in the person. These evil spirits operate through human beings. **"...the spirit that now worketh in the children of disobedience"** (Ephesians 2:2). People who are not filled and controlled by the Holy Spirit are controlled by the power of Satan. The fruits of the Holy Spirit are love, joy, peace, longsuffering, gentleness, goodness, faith, meekness and temperance (Galatians 5:22-23). Perhaps prisons would not be so full and marriages ending in divorce if we engaged in effective battle with the real enemy. Nowhere is it written that we wrestle with our spouse, children, family members, and or people in general. It is clearly stated that we wrestle with Principalities, Powers, Rulers of the Darkness of this world and Spiritual Wickedness in high places. We are wrestling with invisible forces that are real, powerful and destructive. Understanding these four invisible spirits are key in understanding our opponent in spiritual warfare.

The Greek word for principality is *arche*. It means chief or ruler. Principalities are the highest in the hierarchy of Satan's army. Principalities have authority over nations and cities. These are among the first in a high order of evil spirits. Principalities exercise their power and influence over men and women in government positions for making decisions for nations. These institutions were originally established for our good and to bring order and authority to the world.

> **"Let every soul be subject unto the higher powers. For there is no power but of God: the powers that be are ordained of God. Whosoever therefore resisteth the power, resisteth the ordinance of God: and they that resist shall receive to themselves damnation. For rulers are not a terror to good works, but to the evil. Wilt thou then not be afraid of the power? do that which is good, and thou shalt have praise of the same: For he is the minister of God to thee for good. But if thou do that which is evil, be afraid; for he beareth not the sword in vain: for he is the minister of God, a revenger to execute wrath upon him that doeth evil"** (Romans 13:1-4)

Institutions includes government, law enforcement, education, banking, religion, medicine, politics, and media, but what happens when Satan and his demons gain control over these institution? What happens when Satan and his demons dominate government and these other institutions? Once a principality gains control over a leader, or a person who has influence over a large amount of people, it has easy access to everyone under the control of that leader or person. Their objective is to give orders to the Powers. They are responsible for many of the ungodly laws that have been passed, which have a significant influence on world today.

The world has a way of doing things. The world's way of doing things is different from what God expects from us.

Principalities operate through many of the world leaders to establish and oversee laws that encourage and normalize beliefs and behavior that go against the will of God for our life. This is why we are told to, **"Love not the world neither the things that are in the world"** (1 John 2:14). Principalities work behind the scenes to control and influence people. Renewing your mind to the will of God for every area of your life will help you to live the life that God intended for you and will keep you in His perfect will. Many laws are continuously being passed that go against God's will for us.

The media is used to perpetuate, encourage and promote, sexual immorality, use of drugs and alcohol, envy, strife, hatred, unforgiveness, murder, and many other forms of wickedness through media and television programs. Why do you think they call television shows programs? Who are they programming? Pay attention to what you allow to enter into your mind. When you know the will and plan of God for your life, these influences will not have any effect on you. It does not matter how many laws they pass. If those laws or beliefs are contrary to the word of God, reject them. Just because a law is passed to legalize behavior does not make it right in the sight of God. Many people are being misled and deceived into behavior and belief systems that are contrary to the will of God. **"And be not conformed to this**

world…" (Romans 12:2). God is telling us not to conform to the patterns, behavior, or ways of the world. Do not act like them; do not copy their behavior. Do not imitate the world.

The Greek word for power is *exousia*, which means conferred authority. The word power means one who possesses authority or influence. Powers have authority over specific states or territory in a country. They keep control of entire cities. Powers seek to control the thinking and belief system of mankind. They are the second in the chain of command in Satan's army and give orders to Spiritual Wickedness in High Places. Let God be the one who influence your thoughts and beliefs as you renew your mind in the word of God.

Rulers of darkness in the Greek mean *Kosmokrateros*, which means World Rulers. Their objective is to promote false religion and occult practices. They control by deception through false teaching.

The Greek word for wickedness is *poneria* and means depravity and particularly in the sense of malice and mischief of plots and sins. Spiritual wickedness is the lowest of the hierarchy of the demonic forces in Satan's army. They target individuals. The strongman oversees the spirit of wickedness. These evil spirits operate in the form of strongholds that harasses, torment and hold captives those who fall victim. These demons possess and control people. In Mark 5:1-15, a story is told about a man who was possessed by a devil:

"And when he was come out of the ship, immediately there met him out of the tombs a man with an unclean spirit, Who had his dwelling among the tombs; and no man could bind him, no, not with chains: Because that he had been often bound with fetters and chains, and the chains had been plucked asunder by him, and the fetters broken in pieces: neither could any man tame. And always, night and day, he was in the mountains, and in the tombs, crying, and cutting himself with stones. But when he saw Jesus afar off, he ran and worshipped him, And cried with a loud voice, and said, What have I to do with thee, Jesus, thou Son of the most high God? I adjure thee by God, that thou torment me not. For he said unto him, Come out of the man, thou unclean spirit. And he asked him, What is thy name? And he answered, saying, My name is Legion: for we are many. And he besought him much that he would not send them away out of the country. Now there was there nigh unto the mountains a great herd of swine feeding. And all the devils besought him, saying, Send us into the swine, that we may enter into them. And forthwith Jesus gave them leave. And the unclean spirits went out, and entered into the swine: and the herd ran violently down a steep place into the sea, (they were about two thousand;) and were choked in the sea. And they that fed the swine fled, and told it in the city, and in the country. And they went out to see what it was that was

done. And they come to Jesus, and see him that was possessed with the devil, and had the legion, sitting, and clothed, and in his right mind: and they were afraid."

The fight is not with people but with spiritual, unseen, invisible, real forces that operate inside of people that come to ultimately destroy us. Do not make yourself available to Satan and his host of demons. Your body is the temple of God. Satan is using so many people. Decide today that you will not allow your mind or body to be controlled by Satan.

What weapons do we use, and where can we find them? Man can not make the weapons that the Lord has given to us; they are spiritual. These weapons are invisible but yet extremely powerful. In fact, only God's weapons are powerful enough to pull down strongholds. Medicine cannot pull down strongholds. You have offensive and defensive weapons. These weapons include but are not limited to truth, righteousness, peace, faith, salvation, Spirit and prayer. Most people do not consider these as weapons at all. Ephesians 6:14-18 tells us how to how to dress for this battle and how to apply each weapon.

"Stand therefore, having your loins girt about with truth, and having on the breastplate of right-eousness; And your feet shod with the preparation of the gospel of peace; Above all, taking the shield of

faith, wherewith ye shall be able to quench all the fiery darts of the wicked. And take the helmet of salvation, and the sword of the Spirit, which is the word of God: Praying always with all prayer and supplication in the Spirit, and watching thereunto with all perseverance and supplication for all saints;"

Armour of God

Wherefore take unto you the whole armour of God, that ye may be able to withstand in the evil day, and having done all, to stand (Ephesians 6:13 KJV).

←——— Helmet of Salvation
(Ephesians 6:17)

Breastplate of Righteousness
(Ephesians 6:14)

Belt of Truth
(Ephesians 6:14)

Shield of Faith
(Ephesians 6:16)

Sword of the Spirit
(Ephesians 6:17)

Feet of Peace
(Ephesians 6:15)

At first and to the carnal mind, these weapons do not appear to have any power. Another powerful weapon that did not seem powerful at first was Moses' rod. **"And the Lord said unto him, what is that in thine hand? And he said, A rod. And he said, Cast it on the ground, And he cast it on the ground, and it became a serpent..."** (Exodus 4:2-3). God used Moses' rod in a great way and when Mosses uses it by faith, it become mighty through God to demonstrating the power of God:

- to confront the Egyptian soothsayers: Exodus 7:12.

- to turn the waters of Egypt to blood: Exodus 7:17-20

- to bring forth the plague of frogs: Exodus 8:5

- to bring forth the plague of lice: Exodus 8:16

- to bring forth the plague of thunder and hail: Exodus 9:23

- to call and east wind that blew in the plague of locusts: Exodus 10:13

- to part the Red Sea : Exodus 14:16

- to cause the Red Sea to come together again, drowning Pharaoh and his army: Exodus 14:27

- to bring water from a rock in the desert: Exodus 17:5

- to bring victory over the Amalekites: Exodus 17:9

Use the weapons that God gave you! Your faith in God's word will activate your weapons. Truth comes as we continually renew our minds with the will of God for our lives. Renewing our minds to the word of God also brings about peace. The breastplate covers your heart. The breastplate of righteousness strengthens and protects your heart against the lies and attacks of the enemy. Faith brings powerful results. Without it, you will not be able to manifest God's word and power in your life. We are told in Hebrews 1 that faith comes by hearing. We must read and hear the word of God in order to have faith and believe God's promises. The helmet of salvation is the doctrine of the word that keeps you walking as you are continually renewed in your mind and spirit. The sword of the Spirit is the word of God, and it is intended to be used as an offensive weapon against the enemy. Below includes some other benefits of each weapon:

1. **Weapon of Truth**: Destroys lies

    - truth comes as we continually renew our minds with the word of God

    - destroys the lies of the devil

    - the Holy Spirit uses the truth (God's Word) to guide us in whatever circumstances we're in

    - God's word reveals truth that helps us decisively recognize the devil's lies

    - protects us from strongholds, snares, captivity

    - keeps us free

    - keeps our mind new

    - revels God's will and plan for our lives

    - transforms us

2. **Weapon of Righteousness**: covers our body with the righteousness of God.

    - protects our heart and emotions

    - keeps us surrounded by the Angles of the Lord

- allows us to come boldly to the throne to obtain mercy and receive grace from God

3. **Weapon of Gospel of Peace**: provides us with the confidence to face unknown situations knowing that God will not allow our foot to slip or be moved.

  - gives us the stability, promptness and readiness we'll need to face our enemies

  - comes as we study the Bible and memorize key scriptures

  - brings us comfort and assurance

  - assures us victory over our enemy

  - empowers and strengthens us to keep going when we are tempted to give up

4. **Weapon of Faith**: Renews and Reprogram our subconscious mind

  - keeps us safe when all else fails

  - keeps use safe no matter what comes our way

  - stops the lies and evil suggestions of the enemy

  - protects us against the fiery darts (wrong thought)

  - increases as we continue to hear the word of God

  - helps us to obey God's word

  - empowers us to trust God's word as truth

- causes us to believe God will provide for our needs

- protects us from the wicked, our enemies and foes

- causes us to believe that God lives in us, even though we may not see him

5. **Weapon of Salvation**: The mind is the control center which decides if we will sin or not. Protects our mind from the enemy's attacks.

   - protects our mind and thoughts

   - Protects us from and alerts us from false doctrines

   - protects our minds

   - allows us to focus our thoughts on God instead of sinful things:

6. **Weapon of the Sword of the Spirit**: The Sword of the Spirit is a powerful weapon. The sword is formed by speaking God's word.

   - defensive Weapon (blocks the swing of the enemy's weapon)

   - an offensive weapon

   - is the word of God

   - speaking scripture aloud raises a spiritual sword in the air that alerts Satan that you are armed and dangerous.

- destroys strongholds

- empowers us to respond to all negative thoughts with the word of God

- cuts the devil when the word is spoken because that is what is sword is designed to do

- destroy the power of the devil

- **"For the word of God is quick, and powerful, and sharper than any two-edged sword, piercing even to the dividing asunder of soul and spirit, and of the joints and marrow, and is a discerner of the thoughts and intents of the heart"** (Hebrew 4:12)

7. **Weapon of Prayer**:

- brings God into our lives with power

- takes our case directly before God

For the weapons that we use are God's weapons. Let us not be deceived about the power of God's weapons. Whenever you are tempted to retaliate or use revenge on someone, consider that revenge is not a weapon from God. Revenge is about personal retaliation and is a principal of darkness. In Romans 12:19, here is what God, himself, said about revenge, **"Dearly beloved, avenge not yourselves, but rather give place unto wrath: for it is written, Vengeance is mine; I will repay, saith the Lord."** God tells us to be still and know that he is God (Psalms 46:10). God is a God of justice, and he sees and knows all things. Do not fall into temptation to fight your own battles. Remember Adam and Eve, Moses, the children of Israel, Saul and Jonah and how great their consequence was for disobeying God by doing things their way?

In 2 Timothy, God tells us that the only fight we must partake in is the good fight of faith. This is not as easy as it sounds because Satan is always trying to create situations to destroy our trust and faith in God. Your faith gets stronger as you renew your mind daily in the word of God. Believe what God says and use the weapons that he provides: truth, righteousness, peace, faith, salvation, spirit and prayer, and have faith in God!

Your mind is the place in which the battle is taking place. You have only one mind, but your mind has two distinctive characteristics. Understanding the roles and how both parts of your brain function are key and will undoubtedly help you understand where your beliefs came from and how your belief system is controlling your thoughts, behavior and life experiences.

Chapter Three

CONSCIOUS MIND

———◆———

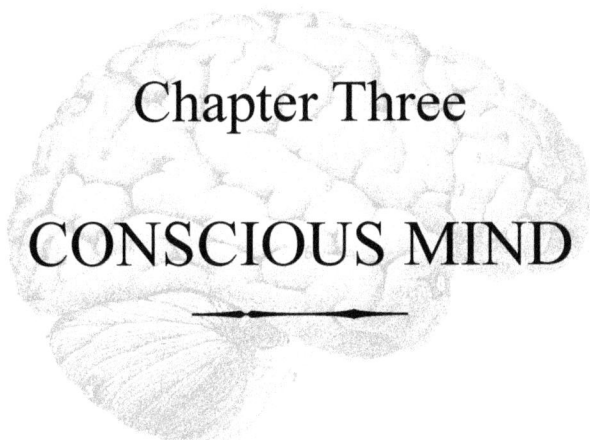

Have you ever wondered why your life has not changed even after you have read several self-help books? ...ever wondered why you have not been able to manifest the promises of God in your life even after you have memorized scriptures from the Bible? Have you ever been frustrated because you feel like the promises of God seem far from your reality? Have you ever wondered why your life has not changed with all the understanding and knowledge that you have gained from teachers, books, audio tapes, and television programs? How can you explain the fact that although you have read many books related to wealth, healing, deliverance, and faith that you are still struggling with these areas in your life? Why is your life still the same? In order to answer some of these questions, you need to understand how your mind works.

Although you have one brain, your brain has two distinctive parts with very different functions. One part is the conscious mind, and the other part is the subconscious mind. In-between the conscious and the subconscious mind is a filter called the Conscious Critical Faculty. Yes, you have two minds, and that in itself is the beginning of a breakthrough in understanding why your life has not changed despite your many attempts to manifest the promises of God in your life. The critical faculty and each part of your mind have different functions. Understanding the different functions of your mind is crucial in discovering the cause of your life experiences, how your belief system came about, and how your childhood programs are still affecting your thoughts and behavior today.

Let us look at the first part of your mind. Consciousness can be described as anything that you are aware of in a given moment. Your conscious mind is where your free will is, short-term memory, thought process, and rational thinking are. Your conscious mind gives you free will to live your life according to your personal desires. Other functions of the conscious mind include:

- part of you that is aware of what is going on right now

- part of the mind that controls all of your voluntary actions; things you do on purpose

- the part of the mind that is creative (because it can think and plan)

- it makes thousands of decisions everyday

- the part of your mind that is responsible for logic: If I ask you want is 4 times 3, your conscious mind is used to figure it out

- the part of the mind that is concerned with the five senses

- the part of the mind that can reason, judge, criticize, analyze and choose thoughts

- the part of the mind that can accept or reject any thought or idea

- choices and decisions are made in this part of the mind

- you use this part of the mind the 5%-10% of the time

- the part of the mind where all of your hopes wishes and desires are

- part of the mind that represents you, who you are and what you want, opposed to the programs that you learned and acquired from other people

- the part of the mind you use in the physical world opposed to the spiritual world

- can reason {find excuses for why it does not believe something}

- the part of the mind that is carnal

- part of the mind that learns from teachers, books, videos, and various programs

The conscious mind is the part of the mind that you are using right now to read this book. Your conscious mind is aware of everything that goes on in and around you. Before I learned about the functions of the conscious and subconscious mind, like so many others, I thought that I was 100%, fully in control of my life. Scientist tell us that about 5% to 10% of our lives is controlled by the conscious part of our mind, which means that 5% - 10% of the time is when you are consciously "in charge" and living out of your personal desires. On the other hand, 90 - 95% of your life is coming from the other part of your mind, the subconscious mind, the part of the mind that you are not aware of.

The critical faculty serves as a gatekeeper, which prevents many thoughts, including good ones, from coming in. the Critical Faculty and the conscious mind work together to evaluate and filter information and statements to determine if they are accurate. It monitors everything that comes into your conscious mind and decides what gets through to your subconscious mind and what does not get through. It will reject any thought that does not agree with what is already in your belief system, permanent memory or programs. The critical faculty protects the subconscious mind and filters out all information that does not fit in or agree with your belief system. This filter monitors and evaluates everything that tries to come into your subconscious mind. This filter is important because once a belief is accepted by the subconscious mind, it becomes a reality in a person's life. Although the filter can be an important source of protection for the subconscious mind, it will reject any belief that does not resonate with what is already in the subconscious mind. If you want your conscious mind and subconscious mind to agree, you must teach them in the unique way in which they learn. The conscious mind learns from books, teachers, videos and programs. It can accept or reject any thought, but the subconscious mind does not learn in that way. This is why you read, understand and learn but still your life stays the same. Our conscious mind, the part of the brain that we use 5% - 10% of the time, is not responsible for storing our beliefs. Your beliefs literally create your reality. Your life is not going to change because you occasionally read scriptures and have positive thoughts if the subconscious mind does not agree with those thoughts. This is a powerful example of why it is almost impossible for many people to realize the promises of God in their lives and another reason why God tells us to train our thoughts and make them line up with his word. **"... and bringing into captivity every thought to the obedience of Christ"** (2 Corinthians 10:5). In order to make God's promises a reality in our lives, we must reprogram our subconscious mind and train it to believe the word of Christ.

So, how do we do this? This can be done in the way that God tells us to do it, which is though repetition and reinforcement as we read, confess, and believe scriptures over and over until they becomes a reality in our lives. Mediating God's word and confessing it over and over allows us to bypass the critical faculty. When our subconscious mind is repeatedly told by conscious mind that a certain belief is true, it will start acting that way by turning that belief into reality, which is the job of the subconscious mind. Your subconscious mind will make whatever you believe a reality, which is what makes your subconscious mind so powerful. On the other hand, if a person believes they are ugly, the critical faculty will reinforce that belief and reject any thought or information to the contrary. It is a person's beliefs that will breed thoughts and experiences that match what they already believe. In order for this person to change his beliefs, he must get the subconscious mind to believe and agree with a positive belief. In this case, a belief such as: I am fearfully and wonderfully made needs to be programmed and accepted into the subconscious mind. In order for this to happen, this statement must get through the filter, the critical faculty, that monitors information, and be accepted into the subconscious mind. The subconscious must agree with the conscious mind in order for this new belief to become a part of his belief system.

Up until the age of about 7, you were involuntarily programed with coded instruction that shaped your beliefs and behaviors. Unconsciously, without your consent, you acquired many beliefs and behavior patterns that you did not have any control over. They did not come from you. It did not matter whether you agreed or not. You inherited many beliefs and behaviors that continue to influence your life for greater or for worse, but there is good news. You can change or replace negative beliefs that have been embedded and frozen in your mind by repetition and reinforcement of repeating new beliefs.

The conscious mind and the subconscious mind do not operate in the same way. Although our conscious mind is filled with knowledge, that knowledge and information have no impact on your subconscious mind. For example, your conscious mind is educated and very smart because it learns from teachers, books, videos, audios, and television programs, but your subconscious mind learns from hypnosis or repetition. In order to help your subconscious mind received what is in your conscious mind, you must teach it in the way that it learns. You read all the books. You listened to all the audio tapes on wealth, healing, deliverance and faith but that information that you "learned" has no effect on your subconscious mind, which learns primarily through repetition.

Your conscious mind is not designed to manifest the positive thoughts and promises of God that you read in scripture because the conscious mind is able to reason. The Greek translation for reason is logos, which means the inward thought itself, a reckoning, a regard, a reason. The word carnal is translated from the Greek word *sãrkikos*, which literally means fleshly and is defined as flesh governed by human nature instead of the Spirit of God. **"...the carnal mind is enmity against God: for it is not subject to the law of God, neither indeed, can be"** (Romans 8:6-7). A carnal mind that is enmity against God means that the carnal mind is an enemy of God. How can your mind be an enemy of God? The problem with our conscious mind is that it does not, will not and cannot automatically accept God's word and promises as truth and will, unless those beliefs are supported by the subconscious mind, automatically reject any statement of positive belief that it is not currently experiencing. The word of God is not intended to be analyzed; we must believe and accept each promise by faith if we want it to become a reality in our life. The conscious and subconscious mind do not function in the same because God designed it that way!

Yes, God made both parts of your mind, and He created them to function exactly as they do for a reason. If you want to make the promises of God a reality in your life, see yourself living the promise and confess it out loud as often as you can, even if it takes an entire year, until it becomes a reality in your life. Usually, the reason beliefs and thoughts have been accepted as true by the subconscious is because of a great amount of repetition. There are no shortcuts to access the kingdom promises of God. You must do as God told us and that is renew YOUR mind in the word of God, daily.

Renewing the mind daily keeps your mind new. God did not make a mistake when he made your mind to operate in this way. He made it this way so that you will depend on Him and Him alone. Some people may never fully transfer the promises of God into their subconscious mind and make them part of their belief system and reality because they do not make their thoughts obey Christ. Below includes an illustration that shows how our conscious mind tries to communicate with the subconscious mind using positive thinking.

Tug of War in the Minds

Your conscious mind says and believes one thing (I am blessed and highly favored), but your subconscious mind does not agree. Every statement and everything that you say or is said to you will be filtered, rejected and kicked out if the two minds do not agree. The subconscious mind is where your beliefs and permanent memory are stored. The number one job of your subconscious mind is personal security and protection of the subconscious mind. It will keep anything out that does not belong there. Your subconscious mind is designed to turn your beliefs into a reality. If what you say does not match what you believe, those statements will be filtered by the critical faculty, kicked out and rejected.

Conflict in the Mind

If I said something to you that was not true, your conscious mind would filter that statement to determine whether it agrees with the statement or not. If the subconscious mind does not agree with the statement, the statement isn't allowed to enter into your belief system or your permanent memory.

Your CONSCIOUS Mind Says....	**Critical Faculty** Filters and keeps things out that do not belong there. It governs information that is attempting to be transferred to the subconscious mind. SECURITY	Your SUB-CONSCIOUS Mind Says & Believes...
But my God shall provide all your need according to his riches in glory… (Philippians 4:19)		We do not agree with that! That is not true! Kick that thought out! Rejected

I am fearfully and wonderfully made (Psalms 139: 15).		But you are sick. You have several health problems. You will never get well. We do not believe that! Do not let that thought enter!
Blessed shalt thou be in the city, and blessed in the field (Deuteronomy 28). The Lord shall cause thine enemies that rise up against thee to be smitten before thy face: they shall come out against thee one way, and flee before thee seven ways (Deuteronomy 28:7).		That never happened to you! You are NOT blessed. You don't even have a job! Yeah right! Rejected

The Lord shall make thee the head, and not the tail; and thou shat be above only, and thou shalt not be beneath (Deuteronomy 13).		What? What is he talking about? We do not agree with that. Get that thought out of here!
But he as wounded for our transgression, he was bruised for our iniquities; the chastisement of our peace was upon him; and with his stripes we are healed (Isaiah 53:5).		Seriously? We don't believe that: Rejected
But the Lord is faithful, who shall establish you, and keep you from evil (2 Thessalonians 3:3).		That is NOT true! Get that thought out of here! Rejected

When the wicked, even mine enemies and my foes, came upon me to eat up my flesh, they stumbled and fell (Psalms 27:2).		That is funny. Reject that thought!
The Earth is the Lord's, and the fullness thereof; the world and they that dwell therein (Psalms 24:1). The Lord is my shepherd; I shall not want (Psalms 23:1).		You do not own anything. Not true! Kick that thought out!
No Weapon formed against me shall prosper (Isiah 54:17)		Ha, Ha, Ha! Yeah right! Rejected!

Because your subconscious mind can reason, it always finds many reasons and thoughts that contradict God's word. It builds or creates arguments about why things cannot happen for us and reasons why God's word will not work in our lives, which destroys our faith and cause us not to fully trust God's word and promises. God says,

"Casting down imaginations, and every high-thing that exalteth itself against the knowledge of God, and bringing into captivity every thought to the obedience of Christ" (2 Corinthians 1-3).

God says make your thought obey his word. God wants us to train our thoughts to obey his word by stopping negative thoughts from sitting around in our mind, remove them and replace them with his promises. This is how you bring thoughts captive to the obedience of Christ.

Our thoughts and beliefs are mainly influenced and controlled by our subconscious mind. The subconscious mind is that part of the mind that has been influenced by others, mainly the people who we have been around the most. This part of the mind (subconscious), which I will discuss in the next chapter, is critical to understand because it is the subconscious mind that was programmed by other people. These programs came with many disempowering thoughts and beliefs that are still affecting many of us today. Programs are instructions, which affect our beliefs, behaviors, and everything that we need in order to survive in the world that we live in today. These programs tell us what to do and how to function in life. The programs we learned as children helped to shaped our beliefs, behavior patterns, and habits. We were ALL involuntarily programed by our parents, family and community and repeatedly receive reinforced instructions that are stored in our subconscious mind. Because of programming, you can take care of your daily needs.

Unlike the conscious mind, our subconscious mind is not the place where our personal wishes, hopes and desires are. Our subconscious mind is not the place that we operate out of when it comes to creating for us what we actually want or wish for ourselves. The subconscious part of the mind represents the myriad of childhood programs, belief systems and behaviors that we learned and when a stimulus or situation is triggered, we replay these learned programs (behaviors): rage, anger, control, resentment, unforgiveness, etc. How did you acquire these programs? You observed, recorded, downloaded, and stored every program in your subconscious mind and replay them when a stimulus or situation is triggered. We all unconsciously learned behaviors that replay or runs automatically when triggered. Some programs include behavior that is: aggressive, argumentative, bossy, deceitful, domineering, inconsiderate, irritating, manipulative, moody, rude, spiteful, caring, considerate, thoughtful, sincere, kind, careless, impulsive. Much of what we learned, from birth until about the age of seven, was below our level of conscious, meaning that we were not aware of many of the behaviors that we learned and automatically replay when the right condition is triggered.

- What do I do when someone hits me?

- How do I react when someone says something that I do not like?
- What do I do when I disagree with someone?
- How do I behave towards people in authority?
- How do I treat others who are different from me?
- How do I behave in school?
- How do I respond to correction?
- How do I take care of myself?
- How do I eat?

According to Dr. Bruce Lipton, author of *Biology of Belief*, 95% of the day, our subconscious mind is playing and replaying programs / behavior that we unconsciously learned from other people. Although many of the programs we acquired from other people are not bad, many of them are negative. What have you learned from those around you who taught you just about everything you know and how to live in society? What you learned from birth until about the age of 7 is still affecting you today. How do you handle conflict? How do you react to stress or fear? How do you interact with others? Those are some of the programs that you learned to help you in each of those situations.

Dorthy Law Nolte, author of *Children Learn What They Live* gives us various kind of examples of programs we learned as children. Some of the limiting programs includes but is not limited to programs that taught you how to: condemn others, fight, fear and ridicule others. These kinds of childhood programs that children acquire from others may affect them for the rest of their lives. A child learns by observing. He does not have to understand what the parent is doing in order for him to learn. Our conduct, be it good or bad, affects the behavior of a child more than telling a child what to do. Children will model and imitate what they see this is why as parents, leaders and teachers, we must be more conscious / mindful of our behavior, what we allow our children to see and what we teach them. In Dorthy Law Nolte's poem, Children Learn What They Live, she writes,

> If children live with criticism, they learn to condemn.
>
> If children live with hostility, they learn to fight.
>
> If children live with fear, they learn to be apprehensive.
>
> If children live with pity, they learn to feel sorry for themselves.
>
> If children live with ridicule, they learn to feel shy.
>
> If children live with jealousy, they learn to feel envy.
>
> If children live with shame, they learn to feel guilty.
>
> If children live with encouragement, they learn confidence.
>
> If children live with tolerance, they learn patience.
>
> If children live with praise, they learn appreciation.
>
> If children live with acceptance, they learn to love.
>
> If children live with approval, they learn to like themselves.
>
> If children live with recognition, they learn it is good to have a goal.
>
> If children live with sharing, they learn generosity.

If children live with honesty, they learn truthfulness.

If children live with fairness, they learn justice.

If children live with kindness and consideration, they learn respect.

If children live with security, they learn to have faith in themselves and in those about them.

If children live with friendliness, they learn the world is a nice place in which to live.

The programs you picked up from all of the people who you spent so much time around gave you instructions for how to live according to their model, and for many, those programs are still affecting their life today because 95% of the day, you are just subconsciously replaying other people's behavior. You can better understand programs when you think about the nature of computer programs. Computer programs can be characterized as a sequence of instructions, a special kind of data that tells the computer how to operate. In other words, the computer program is a list of instructions that tell a computer what to do.

You are the computer and your parents, guardians, and the popular programs that you love to watch were the computer programmers who, from birth up until the age of seven, programed you with a list of behavior instructions that told you what to do / how to function. You were programed to behave in a predetermined way and all of those programs after several repetitions, were downloaded into your subconscious mind and became part of your behavior. Not all the programs we received from our parents, guardians, teachers, communities are bad but many of them are disempowering, negative programs that needs to be replaced by rewriting and renewing the mind to God's original thoughts and plans for our lives. Because of Adam's fall, God requires for us to be born again, and instead of receiving the programs of others, God wants to reprogram us. **"For I know the thoughts that I think toward you, saith the Lord, thoughts of peace, and not of evil, to give you an expected end"** (Jeremiah 29:11). Let God reprogram and renew your mind with his beliefs and instructions.

How can you get the conscious and the subconscious mind to agree? We are unable to renew our subconscious mind by randomly quoting and reading scriptures. Joshua 1:5 tells us,

"This book of the law shall not depart out of thy mouth; but thou shalt meditate therein day and night, that thou mayest observe to do according to all that is written therein; for then thou shall have good success."

How many times do you need to repeat something to make it a reality? How many times do you need to repeat a scripture before it becomes a reality? What does it mean to meditate? According to Webster's Dictionary, to meditate means: "to engage in reflection, to focus one's thoughts on, reflect on or ponder over, to plan or project in the mind." Meditation is powerful and through meditation and saying scriptures or positive thoughts out loud, we can make the promises of God a reality our lives. Meditation is like the water that any seed needs in order to germinate. God made your conscious mind and your subconscious mind. You are fearfully and wonderfully made by God and in order to be transformed and renewed in your mind, you must meditate the word of God. Renewing your mind also restores you into the image of God and helps you to understand who you are in Christ. Do you know who you are? God tells us to meditate in the word day and night because that is a requirement for making the promises a reality in our lives and a way to wash off the lies that bombard our minds daily. There are no shortcuts to accessing the promises of the Kingdom of God. So, how many times do you need to repeat a scripture before it becomes a reality in your life? How long does it takes for a seed to transform into a strong tree? How long does it take before a baby is ready to be born?

Do you get the point? Yes, it will take some work but the more you read and mediate on the promises of God, the closer you get to seeing the reality of the of the promises in your life. Could it take a year and a thousand confessions before a promise comes to past in your life? Is it worth it? If I had to repeat, "The Lord is my shepherd, I shall not want" for an entire year and 10 thousand times before it comes to past, it is worth the download to me. Put some work in and start confessing the promises of God in your life today as often as you can. Repetition leads to a strong belief that will ultimately become a reality.

One easy way to start planting the promises of God in your life is to repeat them when your mind is idle. For example, repeat the following: The Lord is my shepherd. I shall not want. I shall not want. Saying this over and over will cause you to bypass the filter in between your conscious and subconscious mind and help that new belief transfer into your subconscious mind, which will turn that confession into a reality. When you have small moments or breaks in between your daily activities, start meditating and saying the promises of God aloud. Another time that is effective in confessing the promises of God include just before you go to sleep and after you wake up. There are many ways to renew your mind. Although reading the Bible is the primary way to renew your mind, here are other ways that you can begin this process of renewing the mind: attend church and Bible study regularly, read spiritual books, listen to praise and worship music, listen to messages that can help you in areas that you may be struggling in or want to know more about, and surround yourself with things that inspire and motivate you to greatness.

In order for the things that "YOU" want to come to past, mediating and repeatedly confessing the promises of God, are important steps in turning the promises into a reality in your life. Meditating the word of God helps to renew your mind. Plant God's word, which is like precious seeds, in your heart and tend to that word as often as you can. See your heart as the garden that you planted the word in. Nourish, feed, and bring that seed promise to life through the law of habituation, which is by repeatedly reading and whole-heartedly mediating the word of God day after day, week after week, month after month, until one day, you begin to notice that the word has taken root and growing in your life.

> **"...if a man should cast seed into the ground; And should sleep, and rise night and day, and the seed should spring and grow up, he knoweth not how. For the earth brings forth fruit of herself; fist the blade, then the ear after that the full corn in the ear"** (Mark 4: 26).

Renewing and reprograming your mind is a critical step to being transformed and manifesting the will and power of God in your life. We must, **"...cast down any belief that exalts itself against the knowledge of God and bring every thought to the obedience of Christ."** 2 Corinthians 10:5. This is done through repetition in mediating the word of God over and over and over until those promises are transferred from the conscious mind into the subconscious mind and become a reality in your life.

In closing, most of us , although, many people struggle with these truths from God, love the idea of receiving the benefits and promises of God, but I would be remiss if I did not state that renewing and reprogramming the mind involves more than obtaining the benefits and promises of God. The other part of renewing our mind is the critical part that helps to keep us strong and stronghold free. Renewing the mind also requires us to do what God tells us to do.

> **"But be ye doers of the word, and not hearers only, deceiving your own selves. For if any be ye doers; he is like unto a man beholding his natural face in a glass. For he beholdeth himself, and goeth his way, and straightway forgetteth what manner of man he was. But whoso looketh into the perfect law of liberty, and continue therein, he being not a forgetful hearer but a doer of the word, this man shall be blessed in his deed"** (James 1:22-25).

Renewing and reprogramming the mind is our safety net that prevents us from the pitfalls and snares that are always lurking to entangle and entrap us. Renewing and reprograming your mind is a process that will help you to what Galatians 5: 19-21 list as the works of the flesh.

As believers, we must be willing to submit every area of our lives to Christ. **"Submit yourselves therefore to God. Resist the devil, and he will flee from you. Draw nigh to God, and he will draw night to you"** (James 4:7-8). Submitting ourselves unto God means that we are not only hearers of the word but doers as well. Submitting to God means doing what God says in every area of our lives.

Chapter Four

SUBCONSCIOUS MIND

Have you ever seen a horror movie or a movie that made you jump, scream or cry? You know what is going on is not real, but you still show some kind of emotion as if what is happening in the movie is really happening to you in that moment. That is your subconscious mind. Your subconscious mind cannot tell the difference between what is real and what is imagined.

What is the subconscious mind and how does it function? Webster's Dictionary defines the subconscious mind as "the part of the mind that a person is not aware of." It is the part of a person's mind that has ideas, feelings, etc. The subconscious mind is the mental activities just below the threshold of consciousness. The subconscious mind is much, much more powerful than our conscious mind. Below include some of the functions of the subconscious mind:

- The place where your beliefs and memories are stored

- A storage for everything that has happened to you

- Keeps record of everything you have done and what has been said to you, including sounds, smells, etc. The storage house

- Your emotions are controlled by your subconscious mind

- The part of your mind that is responsible for all of your involuntary actions (breathing rate, and heart beat are controlled by your subconscious mind)

- 90-95% of your life, meaning your beliefs and behavior come from this part of the mind

- Keeps the body running

- Regulates all the systems of the body: heart rate, blood pressure, digestion, endocrine system, and the nervous system

- The part of your mind that is always alert, even when you fall asleep

- Cannot tell the difference between what is real and what is imagined; this is why you jump when you watch a horror movie, hear a shot or a car crash

- Cannot tell whether something is true or false

- Is the habit mind, this part of the mind includes all of your habits, the things you do automatically, including the good, bad and ugly habits that you do daily

- This part of the mind is like a storage room of all your life experiences you have ever had

- It remembers everything you have ever thought, felt, done said, and experienced

Up until the age of around 7, this is the part of the mind that was programed genetically and environmentally to help you become a functioning member in your family and in society. Other people, including your parents, family members, community and television, to name a few, programed you to believe, behave and act as you do.

This is the part of the mind that literally controls your behavior and actions 90-95% of the time.

The subconscious mind is estimated to be 30,000 times more powerful than the conscious mind. While 5% - 10% of your life comes from your conscious mind, 90-95% of your life is controlled by the subconscious mind! The Subconscious mind is the part of the mind that stores all of our habits, childhood programs, which includes our emotions, memories, beliefs and behavior that we learned from our parents/ guardians and our environment. A habit is something you learn through repetition. All of your habits are stored in your subconscious mind.

Unlike the conscious mind, the subconscious mind does not learn from teachers, books, audio tapes, and various programs. The subconscious mind learns in two ways. One of the ways in which the subconscious mind learns is by hypnosis. I am not advocating this method to my readers, but it is, according to scientist, one of the ways in which the subconscious mind learns. In Biology of Belief, Dr. Bruce Lipton explains how Mother Nature helped us by allowing a child's mind to be in a hypnotic like state for up until the first seven years of life. Up until the age of about seven, by nature's design, children live in a dreamlike state, functioning on a lower brain wave level, which made it easy for them to learn everything a child needs in order to become a functioning member in the family and in society.

Babies, although they can learn and learn fast, do not primarily learn from direct teaching or from books, tapes and various programs. Instead, they learned by observing, recording and downloading behaviors, beliefs and habits of their parents and those who they are around. The conscious mind and the critical faculty are not fully developed in babies and children. This explains why children learn so fast and easy. Everything goes directly into the subconscious mind.

There is no filter to process, evaluate, prevent and reject information from coming in. Their subconscious mind is open to suggestions and statements that become part of their belief system. If a child has too much negative criticism, he may believe that he is unlovable or underserving because the subconscious mind cannot tell the difference between what is real and what is imagined. Negative childhood programs may affect a person for the rest of their lives. Have you ever heard statements like these?

- He / she is bad.

- Who do you think you are?

- You are stupid.

- You are ugly.

- You are too fat.

- You are a slow learner.

- You will never amount to anything.

- You are hopeless

- You are a dummy.

- You are not good at anything.

- You are retarded.

- I hate you.

- You are sick.

- You will be sick forever.

- You are poor.

- Nobody likes you.

- Who do you think you are?

- This sickness runs in the family

- Your father/ mother couldn't read

- Your mother failed a grade in school

- That will never happen

- Your dad was an alcoholic

- You'll never change

- You will always be that way

- You are cursed

- They all died early

- You are just like your rotten dad

In children from birth until about the age of 7, the subconscious mind and the critical faculty are not fully developed. As a result, statements like these, if repeatedly said to a child, go to the subconscious mind and become part of the child's belief systems, which affects how they see themselves and shape their behavior.

Our adversary, the devil knows that your subconscious mind is always alert. Even when you fall asleep, it hears and stores everything that was ever said to you. It is a storehouse of your emotions, and is often considered our connection to the spirit. Your beliefs, emotions, habits, and long-term memory come from the subconscious mind. Have you ever wondered why you jump when you watch a scary scene from a horror movie or jump when you hear a shot? The subconscious mind cannot tell the difference between what is real and what is imagined. During the first seven years of your life, some things that were spoke over your life were not true, but because your subconscious mind cannot reason and cannot tell the difference between what is real, those statements, if repeated enough times, were accepted as true and became part of your belief system. If you want to change some of those negative programs, you must reprogram your subconscious mind in the way that it learns. Listening to teachers, reading books and listening to tapes will not affect your subconscious mind. Teach your subconscious mind accept and believe the promises of God.

According to psychologists, 95% of your life is being controlled by the programs that you got from other people. You were programmed to believe, behave, and respond to life and people in a predetermined way, much like the people who you have been around or have seen on television. Their behavior and beliefs became yours though subconscious programs. This explains why you like the food you like and why you act as you do. During the first 7 years of your life, your subconscious mind was like a tape recorder. It recorded and stored every experience you have ever had. During this recording storage time, through repetition, you learned, from the people who you have been around, how to respond to life, how to behave, how to have relationships. Your basic programs on how to deal with life did not come from you. They were programed into you by your family. When you learned how to walk, walking became a habit and all the procedures for walking was downloaded and went straight to your subconscious mind. Without even having to think about it, when you need to walk, you simply just get up and walk. It is like push the button and play the program type of thing. Everything you learned, everything you saw, and everything that was said to you during the first seven years of your life was observed, recorded and went straight into your subconscious mind and became part of your life, beliefs and behavior. This is the primary reason why we are told in Romans 12:2,

"And be not conformed to this world: but be ye transformed by the renewing of your mind, that ye may prove what is that good, and acceptable, and perfect, will of God."

Do not be like the world. Do not copy their behavior. Do not become like them.

It is time to start deleting those negative, disempowering programs! Delete! Delete! Delete!

"For I know the thoughts that I think towards you, said the Lord, thoughts of peace, and not of evil, to give you an expected end" (Jeremiah 29:11).

Because your subconscious mind was wide open at birth, this is the part of our mind that the enemy, the devil, took advantage of and continue to uses to try to distort the image that God made you in. God tells us to renew our minds because from birth, other people were able to program us to believe and behave like them. God created you! Although our parents and guardians have plans for us, so does our spiritual father.

After the age of about seven, our subconscious mind learns through repetition. Lipton, hits the nails perfectly on the head when he said, "You cannot change the subconscious mind by just thinking about it. That is why the power of positive thinking will not work for most people. The subconscious mind is like a tape player, until you change the tape, it will not change." Until you change your beliefs, your behavior will not change.

During the first seven years of your life, you were programed to believe and behave much like the people who you were around the most. Children who learn how to speak English did not learn English from a household that speaks Spanish. In other words, you cannot speak English if you only heard Spanish. You learned how to speak and read in English because you were programed to do so. You were taught how to do so. You learned how to speak English because of a program that you received from your parents. You observed and downloaded the program for speaking English, and the language was stored in your subconscious mind and become another program that runs automatically.

Repetition is the second way in which the subconscious mind learns. This is the way that I am advocating for you to train your subconscious mind and how God expects you to turn each promise into reality as well. After the age of about seven, our brain wave is no longer functioning on a lower level, and we are no longer living in a hypnotic, dream like state. By the age of 7, our conscious mind is developed and the second way in which we acquire knowledge and learn more programs are through repetition and reinforcement. Through repetition and mediating on God's word, you can manifest the promises of God in your life. When God tells us to meditate in his word day and night, he was talking about repetition. There is power in repetition. Young children learn what is right and wrong by watching others. Anything can be learned through repetition. Repetition is the key for any learning and leads to excellence in skill mastery. The more something is repeated, the more likely children are to remember it.

Napoleon Hill said, "Any idea, plan, or purpose may be placed in the mind through repetition of thought." Things that we repeat over and over become a habit that is stored in our subconscious minds. A habit is anything that you learn through repetition how to do. Walking is a habit, driving a car is a habit. These two things are things that you learned how to do after repeating it over and over.

Most of us associate habits as bad behavior that one does but anything that you learn how to do is a habit that becomes stored and protected in your subconscious mind. Once you learn how to do something, you do not want to have to learn how to do it again. This is the number one job of the subconscious mind and that is of personal security, meaning that it keeps beliefs out that do not belong there. For example, if I said something to you that was not true (you are a cat), your conscious mind would filter that statement out and not allow it to enter into your belief system or your programs. You would not want to wake up tomorrow and say, I forgot how to drive or walk, or am I am cat?

Once you learn something, it is there for the rest of your life and so are all of your negative, limiting beliefs about yourself and life. If you continually repeat negative thoughts, those thoughts go to your subconscious mind and become fixed idea and will continue to express itself through your actions or behavior until you replace them. The thoughts that you continually play in your mind will move your body into action. However, you can get rid of those programs by rewriting them. Although your conscious mind has the ability to choose thoughts, your subconscious mind does not have the ability to choose thoughts. If you want to change negative, self-limiting beliefs, you must change the programs that created the negative beliefs and behaviors. You must rewrite the programs.

How can one rewrite and reprogram negative programs? This can be done through repetition. Repetition is so powerful that you can learn anything by repeating it over and over. This is how we learn the lyrics to our favorite songs. If you listen to it repeatedly, you will learn it or pick it up without much effort. If you watch something over and over, you will pick up or learn whatever you have been exposed to. This is an example of how programming occurs. According to the law of Association, you become more like those who you hang around or associate with. This law influences our behavior and shapes who we become. You become like those who you spend your time with. If you associate yourself with someone successful, you will be seen as someone success. This is why God tells us in Psalms 1, **"Blessed is the man what walketh not in the counsel of the ungodly, nor standeth in the way of sinners, nor sitteth in the seat of the scornful."** Unfortunately, when it comes to childhood programming, children do not have a choice on who they stand, sit and walk with. Their parents, guardians, family members, community, and teachers shape and influence the beliefs and behaviors of children.

God did not create us to be programed by other people. It was never in God's original plan for us to believe, and behave like all of the people who have had some influence in our lives. Although our parents gave birth to us, God used them as a vessel to transport us into the world for His glory. In Genesis 1:26-27,

"And God said, Let us make man in our image after our likeness...So God created man in his own image, in the image of God created he him, male and female created he them."

God created you in His image and like him.

Like Adam and Eve, our biological parents and family members are not perfect and neither are we. Belief systems effect our everyday lives. People live their lives according to what they believe is right or wrong. Proverbs 14:12 tells us, **"There is a way which seemeth right unto a man, but the end thereof are the ways of death."** What is a belief system, and where do they come from? A belief system is a collection of memories—thoughts embedded and frozen in our minds. A belief system is our personal view of the world. It is what you believe is true based on your personal experiences in the world—a person's reality. A baby is born without a belief system. Most of the beliefs we hold came from other people, mainly our family. We form most of our beliefs about the world when we were younger. The way we were raised influenced our beliefs. For children, until about the age of 7, their conscious mind is not fully developed. Therefore, there is no filter to block out negative statements. Consequently, everything that is said to the child goes directly to their subconscious mind, and it stays there until it is remove with other beliefs. This means that their subconscious mind is wide open and easily programmed to believe any and every thing that is said to them. Do you know someone who is still struggling with or dealing with something that someone did or said to them when they were a child? Have you ever met someone who is still struggling with something that happened to them many years ago? For many, negative statements and negative experiences have been transferred and stored in their subconscious mind and still effect their lives, including thoughts, beliefs and behavior today.

Chapter Five

THOUGHTS AND BELIEFS

Have you ever paid attention to the thoughts you have? Have you ever taken the time to take a close look at the things you are thinking about and saying in your head? If you have not, I urge you to take a moment, sit down and pay attention to the thoughts that are inside of your head. It is like a live movie going on with many characters doing and saying many things. Although I am a fairly positive person, I myself, was flabbergasted once I began to pay attention to who and what I was thinking about, what I was entertaining in my own mind, and what was being said. If you have not already renewed and reprogramed your mind, I am confident that once you examine the thoughts in your own mind, like me, you will be surprised. Psychologist say that 70% of the thoughts we think are negative thoughts. It is time to clean out your mind, bring every thought captive and make them obey Christ. It is time to make your thoughts line up with the word of God. Have you ever noticed that when you try to confess the promises of God over your life or when someone else prophesy or declare something positive over your life the feeling you get? When what you say or confess does not match your reality, one or two things usually takes place. You either change your belief or find reasons why your life is not that way. This is known as cognitive dissonance. This is that uncomfortable feeling that we all experience when our reality does not match our belief or personal experiences. Getting our reality to match our belief or the promises of God takes hard work, but it can be done. Instead of tolerating negative beliefs about our life, we can make the promises of God a reality in our life through constant meditation on the word of God.

We have thousands of thoughts every day. Spiritual warfare is carried out through the thoughts that consistently bombard our mind. Psychologists say that over 10,000 thoughts cross our minds each day. If two out of those thoughts were wrong thoughts, we would have over 700 negative thoughts per year. Thoughts are negative if they cause us to think, feel, act, or say anything that causes us to sin, offended or hurt others. Mahatma Gandi said:

- Your beliefs become your thoughts

- Your thoughts become your words

- Your words become your actions

- Your actions become your habits

- Your habits become your values

- Your values become your destiny

Our thoughts are a powerful, invisible force. If we understand the power of our thoughts and how much is affected by them, we would be more cautious about the things that we allow ourselves to think about. Your thoughts literally shape your reality. When you tell yourself you're not good at something or that something will happen, your mind looks for evidence to prove that and what you believe or think end up becoming your reality. Our thoughts can bring us disease, suffering, wealth, health and death. We have been given the power to choose our thoughts. You do not have to accept every thought that comes into your mind. According to the Law of Attraction, you will attract what you think about; your thoughts create your reality. Not only do you attract what you think about, but you also attract that which you declare out of your mouth:

- I am poor

- I am broke

- I never have any money

- I am lonely

- I am sick

- I cannot do this

- Nobody likes me

- Nobody will hire me

- I am useless

- I am too old

- I am too fat

- My feet are killing me

- This is to die for

- That will never happen

So, if you are thinking about how poor you are, you will continue to attract poverty, and if you think about becoming wealthy, you will continue to attract lack because when you are hoping to attract wealth, you are affirming that you do not have it. Do not allow negative thoughts to linger in your mind; put them out. Do not listen to them!

> **"Finally brethren whatsoever things are true, whatsoever this are honest, whatsoever things are just, whatsoever things are lovely, whatsoever things are of a good report, if there be any virtue, and any praise, think on these things"** (Philippians 4:8).

Whatever your mind constantly imagines or thinks, it makes. Since our emotions are influenced by the subconscious mind, it is not very easy to stop them. However, since we know that the conscious mind processes our thoughts, which trigger our emotions, we can control our thoughts, which will in turn influence and control our emotions.

Our thoughts are as real as the air we breathe. Thoughts are like an unseen magnet that constantly attracts whatever the mind imagines or thinks on. Your thoughts are so powerful that they are constantly molding your muscles into shapes. For example, if your thoughts are cheerful, your face will look cheerful. Prentice Mulford, author of Thoughts are Things said, "If the corners of your mouth are turned down, it is because most of the time, the thoughts which govern and shape the mouth are gloomy and unhappy." Your thoughts are so powerful that they even shape your face and give it its expression. If you want to know how a person is doing or what they are thinking, just look at the message that is displayed on their face. Mulford states, "Our face is a sign which advertise thoughts that is does or does not want to communicate with others."

Our enemy is constantly trying to tempt us with negative thoughts. From birth until about the age of seven, our minds acquired beliefs and behavior patterns from the people around us. By the time our conscious mind was developed, thousands of beliefs, behaviors, and attitudes were downloaded and stored in our subconscious mind and affect our lives and relationships daily. Therefore, many of the thoughts that you think are in some way associated to the thoughts and beliefs that are embedded in your subconscious mind. If those around you had limiting beliefs about life, people and relationships, you may have unconsciously picked up some of those same beliefs. As an educator, I have often experience well-meaning parents who try to explain a behavior or learning condition of their child. I have heard statements such as: My child has ADHD. His dad had ADHD. Everybody in my family struggled with reading. I failed the third grade. I was born with this. He is going to fail, to name a few.

> **"Christ hath redeemed us from the curse of the law, being made a curse for us: for it is written, cursed is everyone that hangeth on a tree: That the blessing of Abraham might come on the Gentiles through Jesus Christ; that we might receive the promise of the spirit through faith"** (Galation 3:13).

Consequently, terrible health and crippling learning conditions are passed down from generation to generation. You and your children must be born again through baptism to receive the nature and DNA of God. In Acts 2:38,

> **"Then Peter said unto them, Repent, and be baptized every one of you in the name of Jesus Christ for the remission of sins, and ye shall receive the gift of the Holy Ghost."**

Jesus Christ paid the price for us and because of His crucifixion and the shedding of His blood; we do not have to endure the sins and sickness of our fathers and forefathers. **"Therefore, if any man be in Christ, he is a new creature..."** (2 Corinthians 5:17). Praise the Lord, Friends! Our DNA and family history do not control our lives, destiny, health condition, financial status, and future. When we you got baptized, your spirit was born again. You are a new creation because you were born again! Your DNA and family background do not determine the direction of your life. Your beliefs determine the direction of your life! Henry Ford said, "Whether you think you can or think you can't, you're right. Whether you believe you can do a thing or not, you are right. If you think you can or think you can't, either way you are right." Do you believe the word of God and His promises? God's plans for us are good; we must renew and reprogram our subconscious mind and align every thought along with God's will, which is the word through meditating the word of God, over and over until his thoughts become part of our beliefs and reality.

The next time you find yourself thinking thoughts that are contrary to the thoughts of God's word, pay careful attention to those negative thoughts and consider who they are coming from. If Satan can tempt us with negative thoughts, if we take hold of those thoughts, he can control our beliefs and behavior. Kyrocos C. Markides, author of The Mountain of Silence explains the invisible intruders called thoughts. He discusses the five stages of sin that come as a result of the power of thoughts. Stage one is called the Assault Stage.

During this stage, you were assaulted with a negative thought. The thought knocks on the door of your mind. This is a fiery dart from Satan. He is tempting you in this stage to take a thought. At this point, this is not sin because it is not even your thought. You have not sinned. Stage two is the Interaction Stage. This stage is much like answering the knock at the door by saying, "Who is it?" You are deciding at this point, should I or should I not? Again, you still have not committed any sin because this is still not your thought.

The third stage is called the Consent Stage. This stage is critical because at this stage, you invite the thought in and decide to commit to what the thought is telling you to do. This is the beginning stage of sin at this point and once you decide to take the thought, you are no longer in control. Stage four is the Captivity Stage. You are no longer in the control once you take the thought. You are now the captive. Sin has set in as you open the door and the enemy comes in to take control. The final stage is called the Obsession Stage. Satan has the key and is now in full control being able to come in and out as he pleases, which leads to ongoing destruction to self and others. At this point, you have given Satan and his demons legal rights to come in, set up and protect strongholds in certain areas of your life.

Although the battle is spiritual, it is real and is going on in your mind. We wrestle daily with negative thought but here is the good news, we don't have do! Yes, this war can finally be over and done with once you learn how to arrest every evil thought. Get every negative thought off the battleground of your mind. Bring those thoughts into captivity and don't let the thoughts take you. No person or situation can cause you to think about something you do not want to. You can choose or reject any thought or idea that you do not like. As you become more aware of your thoughts, you will become more conscious of the fact that:

- Most of the thoughts in your mind are not good thoughts

- Your thoughts control your behavior, attitude, and actions

- You can choose your thoughts

- You can reject any negative thought by replacing it with something positive

- You are in control of your thoughts

- When you have negative thoughts, you create negative emotions

- If you change what you think about, you can change your emotions

- If you change what you think about, you can change how you feel

Once you take inventory of the negative thoughts in your mind, arrest them and make them obey the word of God. For example, a thought comes in, "You are not going to make it." Do not entertain that thought. Stop that thought and remove it from your mind. This is done by first verbally or silently acknowledging to yourself that that thought does not belong there. After you acknowledge a negative thought, replace it with a positive thought, something like, "I can do all things through Christ." As you do this, you are rewriting, reprogramming, and renewing your mind. It is time to remove every negative thought out of your mind. Instead of your mind being a battleground, turn your mind into a beautiful garden by planting the word of God there. Water your garden by meditating and confessing the promises you need, and allow the beauty of God's promises to spring up and become and reality in your life.

Chapter Six

IMAGINATIONS
AND IMAGES

The root word for imagination is image. The Greek word for imagination is *logismos*, which means reasoning, a thought. Webster's Dictionary defines imagination as power to form mental pictures or ideas, to conceive in the mind.

When a child is born, it is no surprise that he comes out in the image and likeness of his parents. A child's physical traits, attributes, and characteristics are passed on to the child from his mother and father. His attributes and characteristics come from genes. Genes carry specific information, codes about specific characteristics. DNA is made up of a sequence of 4 letters. The letters that make up the DNA alphabet are A, C, G, T. The order of the letters instructs your body to develop different characteristics. DNA contains genetic information from your parents and grandparents. Your DNA spells out specific instructions for building everything in your body. In other words, your genes carry the information, the genetic codes, that determine your physical traits. Your genetic traits determine your hair color, hair texture, eye color, eye shape, shape of nose, lips, facial features, length size of your hands, shape of your face, your height, body and all the way down to the size and shape of your feet, to name a few.

Not only do your genes determine your physical traits, they determine your personality and overall health, which includes but not limited to diseases related to mental illness and various diseases such as diabetes, heart disease, and various cancers, which runs in the family. When you go to visit your doctor, this is the primary reason why they ask you so many questions related to your family history and prior family diseases. In addition to inheriting our parent's physical, and personality traits, many of the sins of our fathers were passed down to us as well. Galatians 6:7 tells us, **"Be not deceived; God is not mocked: for whatsoever a man soweth, that shall he also reap."** In this law, we learn that one cannot reap what is not sown; you ALWAYS reap when you sow. This is a spiritual law for better and for worse. If you plant an apple seed, you will get an apple tree. If you plant a lemon seed, you will get a lemon tree. Reaping and sowing fall under the same principal of cause and effect. According to the law of cause and effect,

- Everything happens for a reason
- Nothing in the universe can ever happen by chance
- All actions have consequences and produce specific results
- The choices we make are causes and will produce an effect
- For every effect there is a cause
- For every cause, there is an effect
- This law is immutable, it woks the same way for everyone all the time

There are several examples throughout the Bible that show clear examples where the sins of the fathers affected their children down to the third and fourth generation. A few includes Adam, Noah's son, Ham, Abraham, Jacob and David. Adam's rebellion affected his son, Cain. When Noah got drunk, his son, Ham dishonored him. Consequently, the entire linage of people was under a curse in the land of Canaan. Ham's son Canaan was affected by sexual perversion. His descendants were well known for their perversions in Sodom and Gomorrah. God destroyed the entire city because of the sexual perverse nature of his descendants. Because Abraham fathered his son by his wife's slave, Hagar, and robbed his oldest son of his birthright, other generations were also robbed of their birthright. Abraham also lied to Abimeleck concerning his wife and consequently, a spirit of lying and deception was passed down in his bloodline as Jacob lied to his father, and his own sons lied to him about the disappearance of their brother, Joseph. David fell into sexual sin with Bathsheba and committed adultery. He had her husband murdered to cover up his sin. Consequently, a history of incest, rape, and womanizing was passed down to his children.

Suppose you wanted to make a red velvet cake. In order to make such a cake, you would need specific ingredients. Your DNA is like that recipe (a set of instructions that identifies your traits). Your genes are the ingredients in each cell that is needed to make you who you are. Unfortunately, you have no say in what is written in that recipe. That recipe was handed down from one person to the next from generation to generation with specific instructions for your life. What was handed down to you? What instructions did your ancestors leave on the recipe for you? What is running in your family? What sickness, disease, addiction and or disorders are running around or passed down in your family bloodline that is affecting you, your children and your children's children today?

Psalms 51:5 tells us that we were all born in sin. **"Behold I was shapen in iniquity; and in sin did my mother conceive**

me." Sin is the root cause of all sickness, disease, addiction and disorders and as a result, we bear the sins of our fathers.

> **"The Lord is longsuffering and of great mercy, forgiving iniquity and transgression, and by no means clearing the guilty, visiting the iniquity of the fathers upon the children unto the third and fourth generation."**

This is why we all must be born again. God gave us life, and he has good plans for us. While our parents brought us into this world, because of the sins of Adam, we must be born again and become new creatures with a renewed mind. Although we enter into the world looking like our parents, God is our creator. God is our spiritual father and when it comes to image, DNA, genes, and traits, we are made perfect!

> **"And God said, let us make man in our image, after our likeness...so God created man in his own image, in the image of God created he him; male and female created he them"** (Genesis 1:26:27).

With God's DNA, you no longer have to worry about sickness, disease, addictions, and disorders

> **"Christ has redeemed us from the curse of the law, being made a cures for us: for it is written, cursed is everyone that hangeth on a tree"** (Galations 3:13).

When Jesus Christ went to the cross, he gave his life and he paid for ALL of our sins, wrongdoings, and sickness.

"But he was wounded for our transgression; he was bruised for our iniquities: the chastisement of our peace was upon him; and with his stripes we are healed" (Isaiah 53:5).

When you were baptized a new birth occurred in the spirit, and you became a new creatures in Christ with a new DNA! When Jesus went to the cross, he paid the price for all of our sins.

In this day and age, like never before, the world is filled with negative images. It was never in God's original plans for us to live out of the images that are in this world. In chapter 4, I discussed the purpose of programs. To recap, programs are a list of instructions that tell someone or something what to do. Programs are designed to give instructions for how to perform in various situations. Programs are the basic "how to" instructions for life. They control our lives. The movie called The Matrix is an excellent example of how we are programed to live life from day to day. What is the matrix? Webster's dictionary define matrix as: A mold in which something is cast or shaped. The matrix is man's limited thoughts and belief system. The matrix is man's way of thinking according to the standards of the world. Our beliefs and behaviors have been molded, shaped, and influenced by others. Get out of the matrix and renew your mind to the thoughts and plan of God for your life! God never intended for our belief system to be shaped and molded by others. These programs / instructions that we acquire come from our parents, family members, teachers, community, and media, which includes newspapers, news, radio, television programs, commercials, internet, Facebook, and Twitter—to name a few—that open us up to various beliefs, thoughts, and behaviors that are contrary to the will of God for our lives. Who is influencing you? Influence is defined as: to have an effect on the character or behavior of someone or something. We are being influenced on a daily basis. Those who we spend our time around influence our beliefs and behavior. Pay attention to what you allow to enter into YOUR mind.

Is it possible that the programs we like to watch on a daily basis are programming us to behave just like the people in them? Can you think of some of the popular television programs that people love to watch today? Can you think about some of the top reality shows that people look forward to watching each week? Do you believe that the programs you watch are influencing your behavior? What do they teach us? What are they telling us to do or is okay for us to do? How are their beliefs and behavior similar or different from our own? What can you learn from them? What do they teach us how to do? According the Law of Association, you are becoming more like the people you associate with. When you associate with unbelievers, you open doors and give demonic spirits free reign to attack you. The company you keep could be the very thing that is hindering your blessings, healing and deliverance. Have you ever heard the phrase "guilty by association?" You are judged by the company you keep. Many people are in jail today because of negative influences and negative associations. They are paying for a crime that they did not necessarily commit but because they associated with a person who committed a crime, they too may be seen as a criminal. **"Be not deceived: evil communication corrupt good manners"** (1 Corinthians 15:33). Watch the company you keep because you become like the people who you hang around. When it comes to imagination and images, God gave you the ability to form mental pictures or ideas with your imagination. God gave us an imagination to give us his original thoughts and plan for us so that we could use our faith to believe what he said concerning his will for us. Unfortunately, many people are receiving the wrong images concerning who they are and how they should live their lives. In Romans 12:2, God tells us not to copy or imitate the behavior of the world. If you want to know how you should conduct yourself, do not depend on the world's way of showing you how to live your life. Growing up, many of our natural parents would not allow us to hang around and associate with those who they believed were not good for us. Our spiritual father is the same way. 2 Corinthians 6:18-18, God said,

"...come out from among them, and be ye separate, said the ...and I will receive you, And will be a Father unto you, and ye shall be my sons and daughters."

Some people do not realize that associations can be formed in various ways. In other words, you do not have to be face-to-face with a person to in order for them to be your associate. Therefore, many people are being unwittingly influenced by people who they don't even know!

Programming happens through repetition and reinforcement as we watch television shows. This is why so many people look like their favorite television stars, dress like them and even talk like them. They have been influenced; they have inadvertently become more like the people who they associate with, even though the association is from a distance. It has been said that as much as people refuse to believe it, the company you keep does have an impact and influence on your beliefs and behaviors. Our children are being programed by the programs they watch, and so are we! The programs that many people enjoy watching send many suggestion to the subconscious mind and tell them to do things that led to sinful consequences. In Romans 6:12-13, we are told,

"Let not sin therefore reign in your mortal body that ye should obey in the lusts thereof. Neither yield ye your members as instruments of unrighteousness unto sin..."

The reality programs today are responsible for destruction of marriage and the breakdown of trusting relationships. As a result of watching cold blooded, vengeful characters, many find it hard to trust people. These programs boldly promotes the very things that God tell us not to do. For example,

- Adultery

- Fornication

- Uncleanness (filthiness impurity)

- Lust

- Idolatry

- Witchcraft

- Hatred

- Variance (Disagreement)

- Emulations (competition)

- Strife (Fighting/ conflict)

- Seditions (agitating- troublemaking)

- Heresies

- Envying

- Murders

- Drunkenness

- Reveling (carousing- wild partying)

Any program that embraces and celebrate these things are not from God and is certainly not his plan and will for us. This is an example why God tells us not to love the world. Many reality television shows not only promote these various kinds of ungodly, sinful behavior but they boldly suggest that these are normal ways to believe and behave. They carry negative messages about how people should behave by implanting beliefs and promote negative behavior that influence large populations of people. Most of the television programs have programed viewers with negative thoughts, behavior and have deceived many into believing lies that influence their behavior for the worst. Most people will argue that they are just watching for entertainment, but do not be entertained by such programs that are detrimental to your character and development in Christ. Be renewed in your mind as we have been told in Romans, 12: 1-2,

"I beseech you therefore, brethren, by the mercies of God, that ye present your bodies a living sacrifice holy, acceptable unto God, which is your reasonable service. And be not conformed to this world but be ye transformed by the renewing of your mind, that ye may prove what is that good, and acceptable, and perfect will of God."

Let us cast down imaginations that are not from God and every high thing that exalts itself against the knowledge of God and bring every negative thought to the obedience of

Christ by renewing our mind to the good, acceptable, and perfect will of God in our lives.

If you think you can watch these reality shows day after day, week after week, month after month, and year after year without being effectively programed, you are being greatly deceived. If you think you are not being influenced in one way or another by the various programs, perhaps, there is a stronghold built in your mind that is being protected by Satan. Stop letting the media control your thoughts, beliefs and behavior. Stop letting the media tell you how to live and behave. Get out of the matrix and create your own reality!

"But if our gospel be hid, it is hid to them that are lost: In whom the god is this world hath blinded the minds of them which believe not, lest the glorious gospel of Christ, who is the image of God, should shine unto them" (2 Corinthians 4:4)

Do you believe God's word? Let us renew our mind to what God says about every area of our lives. The book of Proverbs (the book of wisdom) is an excellent place to start for beginners and a great place for experienced believers to reprogram your beliefs and behavior. Let us not deceive ourselves. God wants to transform us in his image and the primary way he does this is though the word. How can so many good-hearted Christians go to church week after week, month after month and year after year without being transformed? That is puzzling and disheartening, to say the least. Part of why we are not being transformed is because we are not allowing our subconscious mind to be reprogrammed or transformed into the image of God.

The people who we directly or indirectly hang around do influence our image, character, the way we see ourselves, and the way we see and view others. This is one reason why we must strive to surround ourselves with positive, successful people. When I first learned about the power of association and influence, I did not have many personal positive and successful people that I personally knew or had time to surround myself with. However, I learned that the same power that is in watching negative programs on television and the same power that the law of association have on my direct relationships could be found in watching positive programs, too! That's right; you can be influenced by authors, books, audio tapes, positive television programs that promote and inspire you to greatness and the lifestyle that God has originally planned for you. Surround yourself with people who have good character, integrity and those who will value you, inspire you, and those who want to see you succeed. Surround yourself with people who will lift you up in life. Think about the company you keep personally and the company you keep from a distance. It is said that you do become like the five people you spend the most time with. Sadly, many people do not even realize that despite the new laws about sexual preferences, new laws that legalize drugs, and alcohol, God is the one who we are to receive instructions from on how to live. Just because something becomes a law or legal, does not make it right. If we based our beliefs and behavior based on the standards of the world, we would not be in the will of God.

"For what if some did not believe? Shall their unbelief make the faith of God without effect? God forbid: yea, let God be true, but every man a liar; as it is written..." (Romans 3:3-4).

Renewing and reprograming your mind is crucial if you are to conceive, believe and manifest God's image and plan that God has for you. The mental picture that God has for you is found throughout the Bible and in the book of Deuteronomy 28 1-13, which include some of the following:

- You are blessed in your city

- You are blessed in the field of your study

- Blessed shall be the fruit of your body- your children are blessed- and everything you own

- Your grocery cart is blessed in the store

- You are blessed coming in; blessed going out

- Your enemies that rise up against you shall be smitten right in your face; they will come out against you one way but flee before you seven ways

- The Lord will command a blessing upon you in the storehouse and in all that you set your hands to

- You are established

- You are plenteous in goods

- The windows of heaven are open unto you and his good treasure to give you everything you need

- Your hands are blessed

- You will lend and not borrow

- You are the head and not the tail

- You are above only, and not beneath

Psalms 139:14 tells us that we are fearfully and wonderfully made. Concerning our enemies and our wellbeing, Jeremiah 20:11 is a power reminder that,

"...the lord is with me as a mighty terrible one: therefore my persecutors shall stumble, and they shall not prevail; they shall be greatly ashamed; for they shall not prosper; their everlasting confusion shall never be forgotten."

This is the image and plan that God has for you, but the devil wants access to your imagination, too! He wants to make a mockery of God's children, God's creation by binding us up with so many stronghold, addictions, and images that do not glorify God.

What is the image of God? What does it mean to be made in the likeness and the image of God? Do you know Him? Do you know His character? That is who we are to like "Be ye therefore followers [imitators] of God" (Ephesians 5:1). How can you imitate your heavenly father if you do not know what he is like? The book of Genesis helps us in many ways to understand the image and likeness of God. Throughout the book of Genesis, God spoke life into existence:

- Let there be light

- Let the waters under the heaven be gathered together unto one place

- Let the dry land appear

- Let the earth bring forth grass

- Let there be lights in the firmament of the heaven to divide the day from the night

- Let the waters bring forth abundantly

- Let the earth bring forth the living creature after his kind

- Let us make man in our image, after our likeness

Whatever God said, came to past. Because we are made like him, anything we say must come past, too. Your words have power. Watch what you say because, for better or for worse, it will come to past. **"Death and life are in the power of the tongue: and they that love it shall eat the fruit thereo"** (Proverb 18:21). Another trait that we see in God is that He is creative. He created everything including: heaven, earth, great whales, every creature that move, every wing fowl. Colossians 1:16 tells us,

"For by him were all things created, that are in heaven, and that are in earth, visible, and invisible, whether they be thrones, or dominions, or principalities or powers: all things were created by him, and for him."

As He is, so are we! Because our God is creative, we are creative as well. I am always blown away about the goodness of God as I see the creative powers working on the inside of me and coming out in my workplace, in my home and pretty much in everywhere I go. God has begun a good work in the inside of you and have blessed your hands and your feet to be creative for his glory.

Another example that shows God's DNA in us is found in Romans 5:5, we are told, **"...the love of God is shed abroad in our hearts by the Holy Ghost which is given unto us."** 1 John 4:8 tells us, **"He that loveth not knoweth not God; for God is love."** As God is, so are we! Because God is love, we are filled with his love and his love is shed abroad in our hearts wherever we go as we show the love of God in how we treat people.

"Every plant which my heavenly Father has not planted shall be rooted up." (Matthew 15:13)

Chapter Seven

CONCLUSION

A stronghold is a place in our mind where negative thoughts, negative attitudes, and sinful habits are protected by Satan and his demons to keep us blinded from God's truth. Sinful habits includes habits that ultimately destroy our life and lead us away from God's plan. Negative thoughts and attitudes include behavior and beliefs that reflect man's carnal ways of thinking. Some negative attitudes and beliefs about life include beliefs such as:

- I am grown!

- Nobody can tell me what to do!

- It's MY life!

- You cannot tell me what to do!

- I will do it when I feel like it!

- I'll never make it.

- I can't!

- You only live once.

These examples of negative attitudes give us a false sense of freedom and led many to painful consequences and destruction.

After dealing with a fifteen-year stronghold of addiction to nicotine, my experience leads me to believe that there are two ways in which one can obtain freedom. The first way is through the power of deliverance. You can be delivered from the power of darkness if you want to be. In Chapter two, the first step in your deliverance includes five things that will help you to begin this process: repent, renounce your sin, resist the devil, for he will surly come back, renew your mind with the word of God, and reprogram your mind with the new, Godly belief.

The second way that you can be delivered from a stronghold is how I was delivered.

"But when a stronger then he shall come upon him, and overcome him, he taketh from him all his armor wherein he trusted and divideth his spoil" (Luke 11:22)

God is stronger than Satan and his demons, and he is willing and ready to deliver you. I was delivered by the supernatural power and hand of God himself. Let God come in and clean your mind of bad habits. Once you are delivered, you will have to make decisions daily to stay free from strongholds. Satan and his demons will come back to tempt you again to see if they can come back to live in their old house—your body. Have you ever wondered how a person can be delivered, clean and sober one minute and then suddenly they are back doing the same thing(s) that nearly destroyed them? Matthew 12:43-45 explains why this happens.

> **"When the unclean spirit is gone out of a man, he walketh through dry places, seeking rest, and findeth none. Then he saith, I will return unto my house from whence I came out; and when he is come, he findeth it empty, swept, and garnished. Then goeth he, and taketh with himself seven other spirits more wicked than himself, and they enter in and dwell there: and the last state of that man is worse than the first ..."**

Satan and his demons will come back to tempt you. Stay away from behaviors that led to strongholds, and do not give your keys to the devil! He cannot illegally come in and steal your goods if you do not give him legal rights!

In 2 Corinthians we are told that we are in a war, **"For though we walk after the flesh, we do not war after the flesh."** This war is not with people. It is an unseen, invisible battle going on in each of our lives, but many of us are fighting people instead of our invisible enemy. How can you win a war if you do not know who you are fighting? How can you win a war if you do not know where the battle is going on? How can you win a war if you do not know where your weapons are? The war is taking place within your mind. Ephesians 6:11 clearly tells us who we are battling with: principalities, powers, rulers of the darkness of this world and spiritual wickedness in high places. We are wrestling with an invisible, evil spirit that wants to ultimately destroy us, but we can have confidence as we use our spiritual weapons of prayer, faith, and the word of God to destroy the works of the devil. Colossians 2:15 tells us that we have the victory, **"And having spoiled principalities and powers, he made a show of them openly triumphing over them in it."** No matter how it looks, and no matter how you may feel, God is with us and is constantly fighting for us. Psalms 34:7 tells us that we are protected and surrounded by heavenly beings, **"The angle of the Lord encampeth around about them that fear him, and delivereth them."**

Although we have one mind, there are two parts to the mind. The conscious and subconscious minds are distinct because they do not learn in the same way. Our conscious mind learns from teachers, books, tapes and by various programs. After the age of seven, our subconscious mind learns through repetition. Up until the age of about seven, we were all programed with belief systems, thought patterns and behavior pattern that are similar to those we have been around. Childhood programs are instructions that we observed, recorded and stored in our subconscious mind that influence our beliefs and behaviors, which controls over 90% of our lives. Although programing is not a bad thing, God create us in his image and like him. God wants us to think like him.

Until about the age of 7, children are easily able to be programmed. Children learn by watching others. Everything that a child sees is recorded and stored in the subconscious mind. The child is just recording and storing everything that their parent / guardian says and do. Dr. Bruce Lipton, says, "Everything you say, everything you do, for the first 7 years of that child's life is being recorded and become their behavior." This happens because a child's brain wave in normal development is in the theta state. Theta is a hypnotic like state, which is a dreamlike state that makes the mind very impressionable and allows it to absorb everything around it like a sponge. It is not that they are so smart but that they are indeed learning quickly because they are just easily downloading behaviors and patterns of those who they are around, including the television.

All of those beliefs, habits and behavior patterns run their lives, and they do not even know it! So, why is your life still the same? Why are you not experiencing the manifestation of the promises of God in your life? If you are trying to figure out why your life has not changed even though you have made your best effort to memorize scriptures and confess them in your life, your life has not changed because 90% or more of your life is coming from the subconscious programs that you received as a child, and they are still affecting your life today. Your life has not changed because your beliefs have not changed. Your life has not changed because the critical faculty between your conscious and subconscious mind monitors and filters out all information that does not resonate with what is already in your subconscious mind.

Your life has not changed because you have not trained your subconscious mind in the way that it learns so that it can believe and accept the promises of God as true. Although you think you are in charge of your own life, the subconscious mind is actually running the show. The critical faculty is the guard that filters information coming into the subconscious mind at all times. The critical faculty monitors everything, including words, statements, affirmations and scriptures that you say and decides what gets to come in to your subconscious mind and become part of your belief system and permanent memory.

You might be wondering why did God make our brain to operate in the way that it does, but God does not make any mistakes. He is the maker of all things and he said that we are fearfully and wonderfully made. God knew exactly what he was doing when he created your brain to function as it does. Joshua 1:8 tells us:

"This book of the law shall not depart out of thy mouth; but thou shalt meditate therein day and night, that thou mayest observe to do according to all that is written therein: for then thou shalt make thy way prosperous, and then thou shalt have good success."

This was not a suggestion. When we mediate as God tells us, we are being obedient to God and honoring his instructions. When we do not do as God tells us, we are being disobedient. Disobedience leads to painful consequences as we have seen throughout the Bible. Some might ask, what is the purpose of meditation? Why would God ask us to repeatedly say the scriptures? Why is that necessary you might ask? Let us recall how the subconscious mind learns. The subconscious mind learns in two ways. After 7, we all learn primarily by repetition. We learn things by repeating them until we get it. Once we learn something, it becomes a habit. Most of us associate the word habit with things like smoking, drinking and all the bad stuff but a habit is anything that you learned and includes the good, bad and the ugly. Repetition of anything makes us stronger at it. It is through repetition that we can distract the security guard that stands between our conscious and subconscious mind. Yes! On a funny note, as we repeatedly feed our mind over and over with God's promises, the repetition is a way in which we can distract and or overwhelm the filter between our mind. This is how we bring every thought to the obedience of Christ. Flood the critical faculty with the promises of God and watch those promises get through that gate and become a reality in your life. Meditation distracts the conscious mind and bypasses the Critical Faculty, or the filter, allowing God's word to pass directly into the subconscious mind and become a part of our new programs, memory, and a reality in our life! Hallelujah!

After the age of seven, your subconscious mind is still recording and downloading the behaviors and beliefs of other people. We are constantly being influenced and under the powerful influence of principalities, powers, rulers of darkness, and against spiritual wickedness in high places. These are our invisible enemies. These are powers and forces that are working everyday causing people to believe lies that influence their behavior. Our adversary is clever in that he uses others to influence large groups of people. Some of the popular music artists are under demonic influence and as a result, Satan is using them to influence millions of people to destroy their lives. The powers are predominately at work and perpetuate their evil through many of the television programs and music that we expose ourselves to on a daily basis. These programs and songs teach and promote everything that God tells us not to do. Many of the programs that we watch daily open doors to Satan and his demons and allow him and his army to legally come into our lives, hold us captive, and steal your goods.

"Let this mind be in you, which was also in Christ Jesus" (Philippians 2:5). Because our conscious mind is able to reason, Romans 8:6 tells us that it is an enemy of God. It constantly finds faults and reasons why God word will not work in our lives. The difference between a fact and that truth is that facts are not eternal but truth is. God's word is true. We must not forget that some facts are temporary and subject to change, but God's word is not temporary and never subject to change. Your current circumstances may be a fact, but God's word is the truth and is the only truth that will ever be. Therefore, cast down every negative report that exalts itself against the knowledge of God and train your subconscious mind to receive the promises of God's word.

Our enemy is constantly trying to tempt us with negative thoughts. In Mountain of Silence, Markides discusses the 5 stages of sin which includes: Assault Stage, Interaction Stage, Consent Stage, Captivity Stage, and finally the Obsession Stage. Our thoughts are the doorway which leads to sin and strongholds. You can control your thoughts! You do not have to accept every thought that enters into you mind. Markides refers to thoughts as intruders. The best way he says to deal with them is to simply ignore them; do not do what they are tempting you to do. God wants us to bring every negative thought into captivity, which means take every negative thought off the battleground of our mind and replace them with his word concerning every area of your life. Replace the thoughts with God's word and remove them from you mind. It may be difficult to keep those intruders out of your mind but keep trying. After you have done if for a while, it will become easier to maintain and manage. Philippians 4:8 gives us some things to keep our mind on,

"Finally, brethren, whatsoever things are true, whatsoever things are honest, whatsoever things are just, whatsoever things are pure, whatsoever things are of good report; if there be any virtue, and if there be any praise, think of these things."

In closing, you must guard your ears and eye gates and protect them from negative images. According to the Law of Association, you are becoming more like the people you watch in the reality shows and more like the people you like to like to listen to on the radio. Do you know who you are? Your identity can not be found in programs and music that promote works of the flesh and ungodliness. Do you know that you were a chosen generation? Did you know that you were a royal priesthood? Did you know that you were a peculiar people? (1 Peter 2:9). God did not create you to look like man made movie stars and manmade famous singers. Present yourself a living sacrifice, which begins by renewing your mind with the word of God.

We were all programed to believe that our genes control our lives. We have been taught to believe that if someone in our bloodline had cancer, sickness, addictions, learning disabilities, or mental illness that we could inherit the same. In Biology of Belief, Dr. Bruce Lipton asserts that that is not true. He explains that our genes do not control our lives; our beliefs control our lives! If we believe that we will get sick, it will be our belief about getting sick that will make us sick. This is supported by the Law of Attraction, which says that whatever we think about is what we will attract in our lives. **"For as he thinketh in his heart, so is he"** (Proverb 23:7). Our thoughts become our words. Our words do create our reality. We need to be careful in what we say about ourselves, our spouses, children and families. **"Death and life are in the power of the tongue..."** (Proverb 18:21). There is power in YOUR tongue! BE CAREFUL not to curse your family with destructive statements. YOUR words have power to bring life or destruction to yourself and to others. You do not have to accept words that do not add to or enrich your life from other people no matter what. In fact, if someone tells you anything that is contrary to the word and will of God for your life, reject those thoughts that do not bring you life by replacing them with God's promises. If you want to know what God's will is for you and your family, it is in the word. God's will is written in the Bible.

"For this commandment which I command thee this day, is not hidden from thee, neither is it far off. It is not in heaven, that thou shoudest say, who shall go up for us to heaven, and bring it to us, that we may hear it? Neither is it beyond the sea, that thou shoudest say, who shall go over the sea for us, and bring it unto us, that we might hear it and do it? But the word is very

nigh unto thee, in thy mouth, and in thy heart that thou mayest do it" (Deuteronomy 30:11-14).

Find the scriptures in the Bible about what God says about your life, future, finance, health, work, marriage, and children and the next time you say anything about yourself or your family member, remember the following scriptures:

- Death and life are in the power of the tongue (Proverbs 18:20)

- A fools mouth is his destruction, and his lips are the snare of his soul (Proverbs 18:7)

- A man shall be satisfied with good by the fruit of his mouth (Proverbs 12:14)

- He that keeps his mouth [from speaking evil] keeps his life (Proverbs 13:3)

- Let no corrupt communication come from your mouth (Ephesians 4:29)

- A wholesome tongue is a tree of life: but perverseness therein is a breach in the spirit. (Proverbs 15:4)

God made our conscious and subconscious mind, and he made them to function exactly the way in they do for a reason. God wants us to depend on Him and Him alone. Renewing your mind is more than just a onetime process. Renewing your mind is a daily process. Walking in the fullness and power of God requires a daily renewing of the mind. Keep your mind new and refreshed in God's word. Get out the of the matrix, which is man's carnal thinking and rewrite the programs in your mind as you continue to discover the truth and will of God for your life. Update and reprogram your mind to God's instructions and promises. If God says meditate on his word, that is his will for us. That is what He wants us to do. Most people try to find short cuts today, and God knows that, too. There are no shortcuts to access the kingdom promises of God. In order to strengthen YOUR faith, you are going to have to mediated on God's word. Renew your mind and build your faith by reading the word of God. How do you develop and strengthen your faith? **"So than faith cometh by hearing and hearing by the word of God"** (Romans 10:17). Faith is another word for believe. Your critical faculty, which is the gatekeeper, filters every statement, scripture, affirmation, and everything that is said to you for your protection. Any statement, scripture, affirmation or spoken word that does not match your subconscious belief will be kicked out and rejected. This is why repetition and meditation are critical components in helping your subconscious mind agree and accept God's promises and instructions for your life. Make his beliefs become a part of your belief system, which will then become your reality. Your conscious and subconscious mind does not learn in the same way. You train your subconscious to agree with the promises of God though meditation and repeatedly confess the promises of God until they become your reality.

RENEW YOUR MIND:
SELF-REFLECTION POEM

"If you want to make the world a better place look at yourself and make the change!"

- Michael Jackson

"I"nfluence

By Stephanie Jefferson

Mirror, Mirror in my heart

show me where I need to start.

Help me look inside of me

so I can be the best I can be.

Positive traits I want to show

to influence people who I know.

Mirror, mirror in my heart

tell me where I need to start.

Wrong attitudes, they must move!

wrong thoughts, I won't approve!

I always influence others in a positive way.

today will be a very good day.

ABOUT THE AUTHOR

At a very early age, Stephanie Jefferson demonstrated a passion for teaching and leadership. Among family and friends, she is well known and respected for her desire to teach and readiness to lead by example. Although everyone expected her to teach within the school of education, no one, including her, expected her to teach, write and minister about the word of God.

A Chicago native, she earned a Bachelor degree in Elementary Education and Master of Art in Teacher Leadership from Roosevelt University where she became a member of Roosevelt's Franklin Honor society.

Stephanie teaches in the Chicago Public Schools and tutors with a passion for early literacy instruction. God led her into the ministry as she attended and graduated from the Living

Word School of Ministry. She is a partner in Faith Ministry Alliance, under the leadership of her pastor, Dr. Bill Winston.

Teacher, tutor, and evangelist with a heart and desire to see people delivered from the powerful grip of darkness to being transformed, renewed in the mind and restored to the image of God. Her ministry was birth out of 2 Corinthians 10:3-5 and is dedicated to setting captives free through effective spiritual warfare and deliverance.

We want to hear from you! Feel free to contact Stephanie Jefferson via email at feedback@RenewYourMindBook.com

BIBLIOGRAPHY

Lipton, Bruce H. The Biology of Belief: Unleashing the Power of Consciousness, Matter and Miracles. Carlsbad, CA: Hay House, 2008. Print.

Markides, Kyriacos C. The Mountain of Silence: A Search for Orthodox Spirituality. United States: Doubleday Books, 2001. Print.

Mulford, Printice. Thoughts are Things. n.d. Web. www.HealingSubstance.com

Nolte, Dorothy, Rachel Harris, and Annette Cable. Children Learn What They Live: Parenting to Inspire Values. New York: Workman Publishing Company, 1998. Print.

www.ingramcontent.com/pod-product-compliance
Lightning Source LLC
Chambersburg PA
CBHW060803050426
42449CB00008B/1518